summer days
& balmy nights

summer days
& balmy nights

simple summer food from sun-drenched shores

RYLAND
PETERS
& SMALL

LONDON NEW YORK

Senior Designer Toni Kay
Editor Ellen Parnavelas
Production Gary Hayes
Art Director Leslie Harrington
Editorial Director Julia Charles

Indexer Hilary Bird

First published in the United Kingdom
in 2012 by Ryland Peters & Small
20–21 Jockey's Fields
London WC1R 4BW
and
Ryland Peters & Small, Inc.
519 Broadway, 5th Floor
New York NY10012
www.rylandpeters.com

10 9 8 7 6 5 4 3 2 1

Text © Valerie Aikman-Smith, Ghillie Basan,
Fiona Beckett, Julz Beresford, Maxine
Clark, Ross Dobson, Clare Ferguson, Liz
Franklin, Tonia George, Jennifer Joyce,
Louise Pickford, Ben Reed, Annie Rigg,
Rena Salaman, Fiona Smith, Linda Tubby,
Fran Warde, Laura Washburn, Lindy
Wildsmith and Ryland Peters & Small 2012

Design and photographs
© Ryland Peters & Small 2012

ISBN: 978 1 84975 207 7

A catalogue record for this book
is available from the British Library.

A CIP record for this book is available
from the Library of Congress.

Printed and bound in China.

Notes

• All spoon measurements are level, unless otherwise stated.
• Eggs are medium unless otherwise specified. Uncooked or partially cooked eggs should not be served
to the very old, frail, young children, pregnant women or those with compromised immune systems.
• When a recipe calls for the grated zest of lemons or limes or uses slices of fruit, buy unwaxed fruit and
wash well before using. If you can only find treated fruit, scrub well in warm soapy water before using.
• Ovens should be preheated to the specifed temperature. Recipes in this book were tested in a regular
oven. If using a fan-assisted oven, follow the manufacturer's instructions for adjusting temperatures.

Contents

Long, lazy days...

Warm days and balmy evenings were made for spending outdoors and taking the time to prepare vibrant and tasty dishes to enjoy with family and friends. When the sun is shining and the days are long, what could be better than making the most of the weather and enjoying good home cooking in the great outdoors. This book is intended to celebrate the joy of summer eating and entertaining and offers a wealth of delicious recipes for alfresco food and refreshing drinks.

Packed with recipes from sun-drenched Mediterranean shores, this book provides all the inspiration you need to create memorable occasions. Whether you are having an impromptu picnic on the beach, an alfresco lunch on a sun-dappled verandah or a romantic dinner under a canopy of stars, you will find just the recipe you need here. The book features the very best dishes that Spain, Italy, France and Greece have to offer.

What could be better for summer entertaining than a beautiful platter of light bites to share with family and friends? Grazing Plates offers a selection of meze, antipasti, tapas and hors d'oeuvres recipes – perfect for a lazy lunch or dinner on a warm evening. Try Crispy Calamari with Beans and Chorizo; cooling Tzatziki or refreshing Seafood Antipasti with Parsley and Lemon. When it's hot outside, what we naturally crave is something refreshing. In Salads & Summer Soups, you'll find Catalan Salad with Tuna and Aioli; Feta, Cucumber and Mint Spring Salad; Mediterranean Fish Soup and chilled Gazpacho.

Food From the Grill shows you how to get the best from cooking outdoors on the barbecue. Try a selection of meat, seafood and vegetable dishes such as Tuscan-style Steak; Sicilian-spiced Seabass with Grilled Tomatoes and Baby Fennel or Summer Vegetable Skewers with Home-made Pesto. Food to Go features great ideas for easily transportable picnics, from authentic Greek Spinach and Cheese Pie, to Onion, Thyme and Goat Cheese Tarts.

Alfresco Feasts has simple yet stunning ideas for more substantial fare for feeding a crowd, from simple pastas and risottos, such as Linguine with Clams and Garlic or Fennel and Black Olive Risotto to impressive feasts such as Whole Roast Monkfish or Sisteron-style Roast Lamb.

Finally, you'll find a tempting array of fresh ideas for Desserts & Drinks guaranteed to keep you cool on a hot day. Try sweet treats such as Pannacotta Galliano with Summer Fruit Compote; Fresh Figs with Vin Santo and Mascarpone or Grape and Lemon Mascarpone Tart. Vibrant and refreshing tipples such as Peach and Strawberry Sangria; Vodka Watermelon or Iced Pear Sparkle are all guaranteed to make the warmest summer evenings sparkle.

grazing plates

GREEK MEZE

Spain has tapas; Greece and the eastern Mediterranean have mezethes. These delicious little plates of spicy, savoury and often salty food are designed to enhance the taste of alcoholic drinks and provide a backdrop to a social gathering. In Greece, groups of family and friends will gather together or go out for mezethes, a drink, conversation and laughter. If you are fortunate enough to have a Greek or Cypriot shop close to you, that is where you will find the creamiest feta, seeded breads and typical ingredients, such as dried wild oregano. Present your meze in fresh white and blue dishes and serve with glasses of aniseed-flavoured ouzo or a delicious Greek wine. Some of the best come from the island of Santorini.

spicy baked feta

No meze table would be complete without a delicious dish of creamy feta cheese.

200 g/7 oz. feta cheese
3 tablespoons olive oil
a pinch of dried oregano
½ teaspoon dried chilli/hot pepper flakes (optional)
sea salt and freshly ground black pepper
lemon wedges, to serve

Serves 4–6

Preheat the oven to 200ºC (400ºF) Gas 6. Line a baking sheet with foil. Put the feta on the foil, sprinkle with the oregano and dried chilli/hot pepper flakes (if using) and drizzle with the olive oil. Season with a little salt and pepper. Close the foil to make a sealed parcel. Place the tray in the preheated oven and bake the feta for about 20 minutes. Be careful when opening the foil, as hot steam will escape.

Serve immediately with lemon wedges on the side for squeezing.

smoky aubergine/eggplant dip

1 small red onion, finely chopped
freshly squeezed juice of 1 lemon
2 large aubergines/eggplant
2 ripe plum tomatoes, peeled and diced
1 garlic clove, finely chopped
1 teaspoon small capers
1 spring onion/scallion, chopped
4 tablespoons olive oil
15 g/½ cup fresh flat-leaf parsley, chopped
sea salt and freshly ground black pepper
toasted pita bread, to serve

Serves 4–6

Preheat the oven to 180ºC (350ºF) Gas 4. Put the onion in a small bowl and pour in the lemon juice. Set aside. Prick the aubergines/eggplant all over with a fork and put them directly on the oven shelf. Roast them in the preheated oven for just under 1 hour, turning them over occasionally. When cool enough to handle, carefully peel off the blackened skin and discard it along with the stalks. Chop the flesh and put it in a large bowl. Add the onion, tomatoes, garlic, capers, spring onion/scallion, olive oil and parsley. Season with salt and pepper and mix well. Serve with toasted pita bread for dipping.

Try dipping chunks of warmed pita bread into this hearty aubergine/eggplant dip.

swordfish souvlaki bites

Souvlaki is the Greek word for a freshly grilled kebab/kabob.
These are made with swordfish but pork or chicken work well too.

2 swordfish steaks
sea salt and freshly ground black pepper
lemon wedges, to serve

FOR THE MARINADE:
1 anchovy fillet, rinsed
10 small capers
2 tablespoons fresh oregano, finely chopped or 1 teaspoon dried
1 garlic clove, finely chopped
3 tablespoons red wine vinegar
5 tablespoons extra virgin olive oil

Makes 12

Put all the ingredients for the marinade in a large bowl. Cut the swordfish into bite-sized cubes and add them to the bowl. Cover and refrigerate for 30 minutes. To make the kebabs/kabobs, thread the fish onto skewers, with two cubes of fish on each skewer. Season with salt and pepper to taste. Heat a stove-top grill pan/griddle or barbecue to medium-hot. Grill the fish for 1–2 minutes on each side, until cooked through. Serve immediately, with a little of the marinade spooned over the top and lemon wedges for squeezing.

seafood salad
with dill

Dill is a herb that is widely used in Greek cuisine. Its fresh flavour works well with the prawns/shrimp in this recipe.

300 g/10½ oz. large cooked prawns/shrimp, peeled
2 celery stalks, finely diced
1 small red onion, finely diced
15 g/scant ½ cup fresh dill, finely chopped
2 peperoncini (pickled chillies/chiles), finely diced
freshly squeezed juice and zest of
1 lemon
4 tablespoons extra virgin olive oil
sea salt and freshly ground black pepper

Serves 4–6

Put the prawns/shrimp, celery, onion, dill and peperoncini in a bowl. To make the dressing, put the lemon juice and olive oil in a bowl and season with salt and pepper. Whisk to combine. Pour the dressing over the salad and toss well. Serve immediately.

pan-fried halloumi

Halloumi originated in Cyprus but is also popular throughout the Middle East and Greece. It has a high melting point so is delicious fried or grilled.

4 tablespoons plain/
all-purpose flour
250 g/9 oz. halloumi cheese
3 tablespoons olive oil
2 tablespoons ouzo
sea salt and freshly ground
black pepper
lemon wedges, to serve

Serves 4–6

Put the flour on a plate and season with salt and pepper. Cut the halloumi into eight slices. Dip each one into the flour to coat. Set aside.

Preheat the oven to 130°C (225°F) Gas ½ and put a plate in to warm. Heat 1½ tablespoons of the olive oil in a large frying pan. When very hot, carefully add the cheese slices to the pan, four at a time. Fry the cheese for about 1 minute on each side, until golden brown. Add 1 tablespoon ouzo to the pan and light with a match. It will burn out quickly and when it does, remove the pan from the heat and transfer the cheese to the warmed plate. Put in the oven until ready to serve.

Pour the remaining olive oil into the pan and repeat with the other four slices. Serve warm, with lemon wedges for squeezing.

hummus

Hummus is simple and fun to make at home. For an extra-special, creamy hummus, peel the skin from the cooked chickpeas – an arduous task, but you'll be amazed at the results.

150 g/5½ oz. dried chickpeas or
1½ x 420-g/14-oz. cans chickpeas, drained
60 ml/¼ cup freshly squeezed lemon juice
1–2 garlic cloves
5 tablespoons tahini
½ teaspoon sea salt
extra virgin olive oil, for drizzling (optional)
vegetable crudités and flatbreads, to serve

Makes about 600 ml/2½ cups

If using dried chickpeas, soak them overnight or for at least 12 hours. Drain and put in a large saucepan. Cover with about 3 times the volume of water. Bring to the boil, reduce to a simmer and cook for 1½ hours or until tender, topping up the water if necessary. Drain the chickpeas and reserve about 1 tablespoon of the cooking liquid. Let cool. (If you want to remove the skins from the chickpeas, rub to loosen the skins and discard.)

Put the cooked chickpeas in a food processor with the lemon juice, garlic, tahini and salt. Blend to a smooth purée, adding some of the cooking liquid (or a little water if you are using canned chickpeas) to achieve the desired consistency – usually about 3 tablespoons.

Drizzle with olive oil and serve at room temperature with vegetable crudités and flatbreads for dipping.

VARIATIONS

Roast garlic hummus Preheat the oven to 180°C (350°F) Gas 4. Cut about 1 cm/½ inch off the top of a whole bulb of garlic and discard. Loosely wrap the garlic in foil and roast in the preheated oven for about 45 minutes until very soft. Let cool. Squeeze the soft garlic cloves out of their skins and add to the chickpeas when you purée them.

Grilled vegetable hummus On a stove-top grill pan/griddle or barbecue, cook slices of red pepper, aubergine/eggplant, pumpkin or courgette/zucchini that have been tossed with a little olive oil. Add to the chickpeas when you purée them.

Minted pea or bean hummus Add 130 g/scant 1 cup cooked peas or cooked and shelled broad beans and 2 tablespoons chopped mint to the chickpeas when you purée them.

tzatziki

Greek tzatziki is a versatile dip that can be served as part of any meze platter. It also makes a great salad dressing or accompaniment to barbecued chicken and fish or roast Mediterranean-style vegetables.

½ cucumber, deseeded and grated
2 teaspoons sea salt
1 garlic clove, crushed
150 ml/⅔ cup plain yogurt
freshly squeezed juice of ½ lemon

Makes about 250 ml/1 cup

Mix the grated cucumber and salt together and let stand for 10 minutes. Put the cucumber in the centre of a clean kitchen towel, gather up the edges and twist to squeeze as much moisture out as possible. Put the cucumber in a bowl with the remaining ingredients and stir to combine. Refrigerate until needed and serve chilled.

VARIATIONS

Beetroot/beet tzatziki Add 1 medium raw or 2 bottled beetroot, grated, and 2 tablespoons chopped chives to the mixture. This makes a great accompaniment to boiled new potatoes.

Spiced tzatziki Put 2 teaspoons cumin seeds and 2 teaspoons coriander seeds in a hot frying pan and heat, stirring, for about 30 seconds until fragrant. Transfer to a pestle and mortar and grind to a powder. Add to the tzatziki along with 1 teaspoon paprika.

Olive tzatziki Stir 75–100 g/⅔ cup finely chopped pitted black or green olives into the yogurt and cucumber mixture.

3 tablespoons extra virgin olive oil

1 large onion, finely chopped

4 spring onions/scallions, including green parts, trimmed and chopped

2 garlic cloves, crushed

600 g/1lb 5 oz. courgettes/zucchini, coarsely grated

fresh breadcrumbs made from 4 medium slices of bread

2 small eggs, beaten

4 tablespoons self-raising/rising flour, plus 5–6 tablespoons, for rolling

200 g/7 oz. feta cheese, crumbled

100 g/1 cup grated Parmesan, Gruyère or Cheddar cheese

1 tablespoon dried oregano

3 tablespoons fresh mint, chopped, or 1 tablespoon dried

5–6 tablespoons olive oil

freshly ground black pepper

Makes about 15

Heat the olive oil in a frying pan set over medium heat, add the onion and spring onions/scallions and cook for 20 minutes, or until softened. Add the garlic, fry for 1 minute and remove from the heat. Let cool a little.

Put the grated courgettes/zucchini in a colander and set aside for about 30 minutes.

Put the toasted bread in a food processor and process to make breadcrumbs. Put the eggs in a large bowl and beat lightly. Squeeze the courgettes/zucchini with your hands to extract as much moisture as possible and add to the bowl. Mix in the onion mixture, breadcrumbs, 3 tablespoons of flour, the feta, Parmesan, oregano, mint and pepper and mix well. It should be dry enough to handle but, if not, add a little more flour.

Sprinkle a double sheet of parchment paper with the remaining flour. Take 1 tablespoon of the mixture, roll it in the flour, then make a round flat shape with your hands, about 5 cm/2 inches diameter. Continue until the mixture is used up.

Heat the olive oil in a large non-stick frying pan and fry the rounds for about 3 minutes on each side until crisp and golden. Drain on paper towels and serve immediately.

vegetable fritters

These courgette/zucchini fritters are best made with home-grown, deliciously sweet courgettes. They are a little time-consuming to make, but every mouthful is worth it because after one bite, you'll be hooked. A cooling bowl of Tzatziki makes the perfect accompaniment for dipping.

fresh mussels *with saffron and lemon*

Mussels appear in some of the signature dishes from the northern Greek city Thessaloniki. This recipe is traditionally served in mezethopolia, which are small, informal restaurants where people get together for drinks and light bites. Serve these mussels with plenty of bread to soak up their delicious aromatic juices delicately flavoured with saffron.

1.5 kg/3 lb 5 oz. fresh mussels, in their shells, soaked in cold water

5 tablespoons dry white wine

4–5 tablespoons extra virgin olive oil

1 onion, finely chopped

1 garlic clove, chopped

1 green bell pepper, chopped

freshly squeezed juice of ½ lemon

½ teaspoon Dijon mustard

a generous pinch of saffron, soaked in a little hot water

2 tablespoons finely chopped fresh flat-leaf parsley

freshly ground black pepper

Serves 4–6

Scrub the mussels well, knock off any barnacles and pull off the beards. Discard any broken mussels and any that won't close when they are tapped on the work surface. Rinse and drain in a colander.

Put the mussels in a large saucepan, add the wine and an equal amount of water, cover and cook over medium heat for 6–7 minutes, shaking the pan occasionally, until they have opened. Remove with a slotted spoon into a colander resting in a bowl to catch their juices. If any remain shut at this stage, discard them too. Put the mussels on a plate and cover with plastic wrap. Add any saved liquid to the saucepan and let it settle.

Heat the olive oil in a frying pan, add the onion and cook until softened. Add the garlic and pepper and cook for 3–4 minutes further. Add as much of the liquid from the mussels as you can, tilting the saucepan carefully in order to avoid any sediment. Alternatively, you can strain it through muslin.

Add the lemon juice, mustard and saffron liquid and boil gently for 15 minutes to reduce it. Add the mussels and a generous sprinkling of black pepper, simmer for 5 more minutes, sprinkle with parsley and serve hot.

grilled tuna skewers

Grilled fish is an integral part of Greek summer life and there is nothing more exhilarating than the aroma of barbecued seafood in the open air. These tuna kebabs/kabobs are perfect for entertaining and would go down a treat at any family barbecue or dinner with friends. They are even better served with Tzatziki and any substantial salad or as part of a meze menu with a range of accompaniments.

600 g/1 lb 5 oz. thick tuna steaks, cut into 5-cm/2-inch cubes

2–3 small red onions, quartered

2–3 different coloured bell peppers, sliced into 8 pieces each

5–6 sprigs of fresh flat-leaf parsley, to serve

MARINADE

3 tablespoons olive oil

freshly squeezed juice of 1 large lemon

2 garlic cloves, crushed

1 fresh green chilli/chile, deseeded and finely chopped

1 tablespoon dried oregano

1 teaspoon dried thyme

a handful of fresh flat-leaf parsley, finely chopped

sea salt and freshly ground black pepper

Makes 6

To make the marinade, put the olive oil, lemon juice, garlic, chilli/chile, oregano, thyme, parsley, salt and pepper in a large bowl and beat well. Add the tuna pieces and stir to coat. Cover with plastic wrap and chill in the refrigerator for 2–3 hours, stirring occasionally.

Separate the onion quarters into 2–3 pieces each, according to their size. Remove the tuna cubes from the marinade. Starting with a piece of pepper, thread pieces of tuna, onion and pepper onto skewers, finishing each with a piece of pepper. Repeat until all the ingredients are used up.

Preheat a stove-top grill pan/griddle or barbecue to hot and cook for 5–7 minutes on each side until seared on the outside but pink in the middle, basting with the leftover marinade as they cook. Take care, as tuna can become dry if overcooked.

Meanwhile, put the remaining marinade into a small saucepan and boil for 2–3 minutes. Arrange the skewers on a platter and top with sprigs of parsley. Serve immediately, drizzled with the leftover marinade.

spicy chicken skewers

Long metal skewers of glistening grilled chicken or lamb with enticing garlicky aromas, have always been a classic feature of any Greek meze table. Ground sumac adds a lemony flavour to these delicious kebabs/kabobs and can be found in most Middle Eastern stores.

750 g/1 lb 10 oz. boneless chicken, cut into large cubes

2 small red onions, quartered

2 red or yellow bell peppers, sliced into 8 pieces each

MARINADE

4 tablespoons olive oil

freshly squeezed juice of 1 lemon

3 garlic cloves, crushed

1 teaspoon ground cumin

½ teaspoon ground allspice

½ teaspoon ground sumac

sea salt and freshly ground black pepper

TO SERVE

6 small pita breads

2 tablespoons fresh flat-leaf parsley, chopped

Makes 6

To make the marinade, put all the ingredients in a large bowl and beat well. Add the chicken cubes and stir to coat. Cover and chill in the refrigerator for 6 hours or overnight.

Separate the onion quarters into 2–3 pieces each, according to their size. Starting with a piece of chicken, thread pieces of chicken, onion and pepper onto a skewer, then repeat until all the ingredients are used up.

Preheat a stove-top grill pan/griddle or barbecue to hot and cook for 8–10 minutes on each side until golden and cooked through, turning frequently.

Split the pita breads along one side and heat them on the barbecue or under the grill/broiler. Sprinkle the chicken skewers with parsley and serve immediately with the hot pita breads.

VARIATION

Lamb skewers Add 1 teaspoon ground coriander and 3 tablespoons plain yogurt to the marinade, but omit the sumac. Instead of chicken, use 1 kg/2 lb 4 oz. boneless lamb (preferably leg meat), cut into cubes. Thread the meat onto the skewers. Preheat a stove-top grill pan/griddle or barbecue to hot and add the skewers. Cook for 8–10 minutes on each side until charred and cooked through, turning frequently. Pull the meat off the skewers and sprinkle with thinly sliced red onion and 1 tablespoon sumac. Serve immediately with hot pita breads on the side.

fried meatballs

No social gathering in Greece is complete without a plate of these tasty meatballs, known as keftethes. The fresh flavours of the lemon juice and the herbs adds a real depth of flavour to the meat and they are always a pleasure to eat. The delicious aroma of these meatballs frying in the kitchen always brings a celebratory air with it, as many Greek families use their own secret recipe passed down through generations. They are perfect served with a traditional Greek salad made with fresh tomatoes, cucumber and creamy feta cheese and a glass of ice-cold beer.

3 medium slices of bread, crusts discarded and soaked in water

500 g/1 lb 2 oz. minced/ground beef or lamb

1 tablespoon freshly squeezed lemon juice or white wine

1 onion, grated

1 egg, lightly beaten

1 tablespoon dried oregano

a small bunch of fresh mint, chopped

5 tablespoons plain/all-purpose flour

4–5 tablespoons sunflower oil

sea salt and freshly ground black pepper

Makes about 15

Drain the bread and squeeze out the excess water, then put the bread in a bowl. Add the meat, lemon juice, onion, egg, oregano, mint, salt and pepper. Mix with your hands until combined.

Put the flour on a work surface. Make round, walnut-sized balls of the meat mixture, then roll them lightly in the flour.

Heat the oil in a non-stick frying pan set over medium–high heat, add the meatballs and fry until golden on all sides, turning frequently. Remove and drain on paper towels, then serve immediately with lemon wedges for squeezing.

pork with quinces

If there was a beauty contest for fruit, quinces would be among the strongest contenders. These beautiful fruit bear the prettiest of flowers and have a lovely golden colour. Quinces are also very versatile and can be used for cooking all sorts of wonderful savoury and sweet recipes. They make a delicious dessert roasted whole in the oven and served with whipped cream, or can be made into preserves or added to casseroles with lamb, beef or pork.

3 tablespoons olive oil

6 boneless steaks of pork tenderloin, about 1 kg/2 lb 4 oz., or 6 leg steaks

freshly squeezed juice of 1 lemon

2–3 allspice berries (optional)

2 quinces, about 750 g/1 lb 10 oz.

4–5 tablespoons sunflower oil

2 tablespoons light brown sugar

¼ teaspoon ground cinnamon

sea salt

Serves 6

Heat the olive oil in a large saucepan over high heat, add the pork and fry until golden on both sides. Reduce the heat, pour half the lemon juice over the meat and let it evaporate for 2–3 minutes. Add the allspice berries, if using, and 450 ml/scant 2 cups hot water, cover and simmer for 30 minutes, adding a little salt towards the end.

Fill a large bowl with cold water and add the remaining lemon juice. Cut the quinces into quarters, then core and peel them. Put the quince quarters in the water straight away to stop them discolouring.

Drain the quinces and pat them dry. Slice each piece in half vertically. Heat the oil in a large frying pan. Working in batches, add as many of the quince slices as you can in one layer and fry over low heat until golden on one side. Turn and cook for 15–20 minutes to brown the other side. Spread on top of the pork.

Sprinkle with sugar and cinnamon and add a little more hot water until the quinces are almost covered. Tilt the saucepan to mix the ingredients. Cover and cook slowly for 45 minutes until tender. Do not stir after the quinces have been added, but lift and shake the saucepan gently instead. Serve hot.

CLASSIC ITALIAN ANTIPASTI

Italian antipasti are a selection of appetizers served as the first course of a formal Italian meal. Traditional antipasti often includes regional dishes that make the most of delicious local produce, including cured meats such as salami or prosciutto, olives, roasted garlic, pepperoncini, mushrooms, anchovies, artichoke hearts, a range of salads and a variety of cheeses such as mozzarella or pecorino. These are often served with a selection of fresh Italian breads and olive oil and are perfect for entertaining and sharing with family and friends.

caponata

Caponata is a classic Italian antipasto dish. It is a cooked vegetable salad made with aubergines/eggplant. There are many local variations of this delicious dish, some of which include carrots, peppers, potatoes, pine nuts and even raisins.

1 aubergine/eggplant, cut into
1 cm/½ inch cubes

1 tablespoon sea salt

4 tablespoons extra virgin olive oil

2 red onions, cut into 8 wedges each

4 garlic cloves, chopped

100 g/¾ cup green olives

75 g/½ cup black olives

50 g/⅓ cup capers in brine, rinsed

2 teaspoons fresh oregano, marjoram
or thyme leaves, finely chopped,
plus extra sprigs to serve

3 medium tomatoes cut into
8 wedges each

2 baby courgettes/zucchini, sliced

2 tablespoons tomato purée/paste

2 teaspoons sugar

150 ml/⅔ cup chicken or vegetable
stock or water

4 tablespoons chopped fresh
flat-leaf parsley

Serves 6–8

Sprinkle the aubergine/eggplant with the salt, toss well and let stand for 10 minutes. Drain and pat dry with paper towels.

Put the oil into a large, heavy-based saucepan until very hot. Add the onion, garlic, olives and capers. Cook over high heat for 2–3 minutes, stirring, then add the aubergine/eggplant and continue to cook, stirring, over medium heat for another 8 minutes. Using a slotted spoon, transfer the mixture to a plate and set aside.

Add the oregano, marjoram or thyme to the pan, then add the tomatoes, courgettes/zucchini, tomato purée/paste, sugar and stock or water. Stir gently and bring to the boil. Reduce the heat and simmer for 8 minutes. Return the aubergine/eggplant mixture to the pan and simmer gently until the flavours have mingled. The vegetables should still be intact, not mushy. Dip the pan into a bowl of cold water to cool.

Sprinkle with parsley and top with the extra sprigs of oregano, marjoram or thyme, if using. Serve warm, cool or cold, but not chilled.

radicchio *with gorgonzola and walnuts*

125–150 g/4½–5 oz. Gorgonzola cheese
1 head of radicchio
1 head of trevise
2 tablespoons extra virgin
olive oil
75 g/1 cup shelled walnuts or pecans
freshly ground black pepper

Serves 4

Slice or break the cheese into 5-cm/2-inch wedges or chunks.

Separate the radicchio and trevise into leaves.

Arrange the leaves on small serving plates, drizzle with olive oil, add the Gorgonzola and walnuts or pecans, then serve, sprinkled with freshly ground black pepper.

Radicchio, the bitter red Italian chicory, is used as a salad leaf and also cooked as a vegetable. The round-headed Verona variety is available all year round, while trevise, the version with long leaves, is usually only available during autumn and winter. If you can't find them, use another bitter green, such as frisée or escarole, instead. Teamed with velvety blue Gorgonzola and walnuts, this is an utterly irresistible combination.

deep-fried baby artichokes

These long-stemmed baby artichokes are fried in hot olive oil with their heads down, squashed out flat like daisies. Deep-frying gives them a delicious crunchy texture and a warm and sunny golden colour. This recipe calls for tiny globe artichoke heads, preferably with violet petals and no more than 5 cm/2 inches long. Try to use the freshest baby spring artichokes you can find for the very best results. It is an unusual dish that is perfect for serving up with a selection of antipasto at a spring or summer meal.

10–12 tiny globe artichokes, with stalks attached, quartered lengthways
extra virgin olive oil
sea salt and freshly ground pepper
lemon wedges, to serve

Serves 4–6

Fill a saucepan with the olive oil to a depth of 5 cm/2 inches. Heat to about 190°C (375°F) or until a cube of bread turns brown within 40 seconds.

Add the artichokes, 6–8 at a time and, using a slotted spoon, push them down hard against the bottom of the pan. Fry until they are crisp and smell caramelized. Carefully remove with tongs or a slotted spoon and drain, stems upward. Keep hot or warm while you cook the rest.

Remove the stalks and sprinkle with salt and pepper. Serve immediately with lemon wedges on the side for squeezing.

asparagus with prosciutto

8 thin slices prosciutto, such as Parma ham
500 g/1lb 2 oz. bunch of thick asparagus
2 tablespoons extra virgin olive oil
or lemon oil

Serves 4

Before turning on the oven, hang the slices
of prosciutto over the grids of the top oven
rack. Slide the rack into the oven, then turn
it on to 150°C (300°F) Gas 2. Leave for
20 minutes until the ham is dry and crisp.
Remove carefully and set aside.

Preheat the grill/broiler to hot.

Using a vegetable peeler, peel 7.5 cm/
3 inches of the tough skin off the end of each
asparagus spear, then snap off and discard
any tough ends. Arrange the asparagus on
a shallow baking sheet and sprinkle with the
oil. Grill/broil for 6–8 minutes, or until the
asparagus is wrinkled and tender.

Serve the asparagus with some of the hot
oil from the grill/broiler pan and 2 crisp slices
of prosciutto for each person.

Asparagus in season is pure delight and, whether it is the fine wild
variety or the large cultivated type, it is considered a particular treat in
Italy. Add the delicate sweetness of Parma ham, dried to crispness, and
you have an unusual combination. Use white asparagus if you can find it
(French and Italian greengrocers often stock this during early summer),
though green asparagus is more usual. Serve with frizzante, such as
Lambrusco, or a crisp, dry, white wine.

seafood antipasti *with parsley and lemon*

Prawns/shrimp are very popular in mixed seafood antipasti. Some prawns/shrimp are striped grey or blue; others have pearly, silvery shells or look almost translucent. This recipe suits almost any prawn/shrimp variety – simply adjust the cooking time slightly to suit the size of the prawns/shrimp. Just make sure they are as fresh as you can get.

750 g/1 lb 10 oz. large, whole fresh prawns/shrimp, unpeeled and washed

2 tablespoons sea salt

1 tablespoon red wine vinegar

4 large sprigs of fresh flat-leaf parsley, chopped

freshly squeezed juice of 2 lemons, plus 2 lemons, halved, to serve (optional)

2 tablespoons extra virgin olive oil

Serves 4

To devein the prawns, cut a slit down the back into the flesh and discard any black thread. Put 250 ml/1 cup water into a saucepan, add the salt and bring to the boil. Add the prawns/shrimp and stir in the vinegar and parsley stalks. Return to the boil, reduce the heat and cook gently for about 2–4 minutes, stirring and repositioning the prawns/shrimp now and then, until their flesh turns dense, white and firm and the shells turn pink.

Remove the cooked prawns/shrimp to a serving dish. Reserve 2 tablespoons of the cooking liquid and put into a small jug. Add the lemon juice, oil and parsley leaves, mix well, then pour over the prawns/shrimp. Let cool, then marinate in the refrigerator for 10–20 minutes.

Serve with halved lemons for squeezing.

SPANISH TAPAS

Tapas are appetizers or light snacks that are often served in informal bars or restaurants with drinks. They can be hot dishes such as meatballs or fried squid, or cold dishes such as cured meats, slices of tortilla, or a variety of cheeses such as Manchego or Castilla. Tapas menus vary widely between different regions, using local produce and ingredients. The word 'tapas' comes from the Spanish word 'tapar', meaning 'to cover'. Tapas were given this name because they were originally served in bars and used as lids covering alcoholic drinks to protect the drinks from fruit flies. Tapas are a tradition that is at the heart of Spanish culture and all over Spain you will find lively bars serving these delicious small plates of local delicacies.

potatoes in spicy sauce

No tapas table is complete without a dish of potatoes topped with spicy sauce. This dish can be found all over Spain, but the ingredients of the sauce can vary from region to region.

10 small red potatoes, peeled
7 tablespoons olive oil
1 small onion, finely chopped
2 garlic cloves, finely chopped
2 teaspoons pimentón dulce (Spanish sweet paprika)
1 teaspoon ground cumin
1 tablespoon mild chilli/chili powder
1 x 400-g/14-oz. can plum tomatoes, puréed
1 tablespoon sherry vinegar
sea salt and freshly ground black pepper

Serves 4–6

Preheat the oven to 200ºC (400ºF) Gas 6. Boil the potatoes in salted water until just tender. Drain and when cool enough to handle, cut into quarters. Place on a baking sheet and drizzle with 3 tablespoons of the olive oil. Season well with salt and pepper and bake in the preheated oven for about 40 minutes, until crisp.

Heat the remaining olive oil in a large saucepan. Add the onion and garlic and cook for a few minutes until soft. Add all of the remaining ingredients, season to taste with salt and pepper and stir as the sauce warms through. Pour the sauce over the potatoes and serve warm.

pan-fried green peppers

These bright green padrón peppers hail from the Spanish region of Galicia. They are a popular tapa among tourists and locals alike.

2 tablespoons extra virgin olive oil
150 g/5 Padrón peppers or other small green peppers, such as poblano chillies/chiles
1–2 teaspoons coarse sea salt

Serves 4–6

Heat the olive oil in a large, heavy-based frying pan until very hot. Add the peppers and cook them over high heat for 2–3 minutes, shaking the pan to stop them catching and burning. As soon as they puff up and start to brown, remove from the heat and sprinkle generously with the salt. Serve immediately.

alioli

4–6 garlic cloves, crushed
1 whole egg
1 egg yolk
1 teaspoon freshly squeezed lemon juice
500 ml/2 cups olive oil
sea salt and freshly ground black pepper

Makes about 600 ml/2½ cups

Alioli is the garlic-laden version of the Spanish mayonnaise, mahonesa, thought to have originated in Mahon, the capital of the island of Menorca. To help stop it separating, have all the ingredients at room temperature, perhaps slightly warming the oil first – then adding in stages, not in a steady stream as is sometimes recommended.

Put the garlic, egg and egg yolk and lemon juice in a food processor. Blend until pale yellow. Keeping the motor running, slowly pour in the olive oil, a bit at a time. Blend well, until thick and silky, then add salt and pepper to taste. Serve at room temperature with fish or meat.

Alioli with potatoes Put 500 g/1 lb 2 oz. unpeeled new potatoes in a saucepan, cover with cold water, add a pinch of salt and boil until tender. Drain and let cool. Slip off the skins, cut the potatoes into bite-sized pieces, then serve with alioli as a dip.

Parmesan crackers

This is a robust savoury biscuit made using plastic wrap to roll the mixture into a log and then refrigerating it until needed. All you then have to do is cut the chilled dough into slices and bake. The inclusion of smoked paprika gives these a distinctly Spanish feel, making them great to serve with Manchego cheese and some Spanish quince paste (membrillo) on the side.

125 g/1 stick plus 1 tablespoon unsalted butter, cubed and softened
80 g/3 oz. mature Cheddar cheese, grated
20 g/1 oz. Parmesan cheese, finely grated
150 g/1 cup plus 2 tablespoons plain/all-purpose flour
¼ teaspoon smoked paprika (pimentón)
a baking sheet lined with parchment paper

TO SERVE
sliced Manchego cheese
quince paste (membrillo)

Makes about 60

Combine the butter and both cheeses in a food processor. Add the flour and paprika and process until just combined and the mixture forms into lots of smaller balls of dough. Add 1–2 tablespoons cold water and process until the dough roughly comes together.

Lay a sheet of plastic wrap on a work surface and spoon half of the mixture down the centre to form a log, about 3 cm/2 inches across. Firmly roll up. Repeat with the remaining dough to make 2 logs and refrigerate for about 1 hour, until firm. Preheat the oven to 180°C (350°F) Gas 4. Finely slice the logs and arrange the discs on the prepared baking sheet. Bake in the preheated oven for 8–10 minutes and then transfer to a wire rack to cool and become crisp. Serve cool with sliced Manchego and quince paste.

red pepper and Manchego tortilla

Tortilla is a hearty Spanish omelette that is often served in slices as a tapa. The addition of cheese to a tortilla makes it substantial enough for a main meal. You may feel it's time-consuming to fry the vegetables separately, but it improves the flavour and texture of the finished dish.

6 tablespoons extra virgin olive oil, plus extra to fry

1 large onion, very thinly sliced

1 large red bell pepper, finely sliced (you can also use marinated roasted peppers, in which case add them at the same time as the Manchego)

350 g/12 oz. salad potatoes, very thinly sliced

8 eggs

75 g/2½ oz. Manchego, thinly sliced

sea salt and freshly ground black pepper

Serves 4–6

Heat 4 tablespoons of the oil in a large, deep lidded frying pan or wok. Add the onion and pepper and cook over medium heat until soft and beginning to brown at the edges. Remove from the pan with a slotted spoon, leaving behind the oil.

Add the remaining oil to the pan, heat for 1 minute, then tip in the potatoes and stir with a spatula to ensure the slices are separate and well coated in oil. Fry for about 5–6 minutes until they start to brown, stirring frequently, then reduce the heat, cover with the lid and cook for another 10–15 minutes until the potatoes are tender, turning them every so often so that they don't catch.

Put the onion and pepper back into the pan, mix with the potatoes and continue to fry (uncovered) for another 5 minutes. Season generously with salt and pepper and set aside for 10 minutes or so to cool.

Break the eggs into a large bowl and beat lightly. Tip the contents of the frying pan and the Manchego into the beaten eggs and mix gently. Heat a clean frying pan until moderately hot, add a little oil, wipe off the excess with paper towels, then pour in the egg mixture. Lift the edge of the tortilla as it begins to cook, letting the liquid egg run from the centre to the edge. Cook until most of the egg has set, then reduce the heat a little and cook for about 3–4 minutes. Meanwhile, preheat the grill/broiler to medium.

Slip the pan under the grill/broiler and grill/broil for about 4 minutes until the top of the tortilla has puffed up and lightly browned and the egg in the middle has set. Remove from the grill/broiler and leave to cool for about 30 minutes in the pan. Loosen the tortilla around the edges, place a plate over the pan and flip over onto the plate. Cut into wedges and serve at room temperature.

prawns/shrimp with garlic

Fresh seafood can be found all over the Mediterranean. The sherry and garlic used here gives these prawns/shrimp an authentic Spanish flavour.

4 tablespoons olive oil
3 garlic cloves, finely chopped
½ teaspoon dried chilli/hot pepper flakes
400 g/14 oz. large raw prawns/shrimp, unpeeled
1 tablespoon dry sherry
2 tablespoons chopped fresh flat-leaf parsley

Serves 4–6

Heat the oil in a frying pan. Add the garlic and chilli/hot pepper flakes and cook until golden. Add the prawns/shrimp and cook for 1–2 minutes over high heat. Pour in the sherry and cook for 1–2 minutes further, until the prawns are cooked through. Remove from the heat, sprinkle with parsley and serve immediately.

crispy calamari *with beans and chorizo*

Try to use small, tender baby squid rings with tentacles for this recipe. The beans and chorizo make this into a substantial dish, so it can be served with a simple salad or a selection of tapas.

2 tablespoons olive oil

1 onion, thinly sliced

1 garlic clove, crushed

½ teaspoon cumin seeds, lightly crushed

a pinch of crushed dried chillies/chiles

½ teaspoon dried oregano

100 g/3½ oz. cooking chorizo, diced

200-g/6½-oz. can chopped tomatoes

400-g/14-oz. can butter/lima beans, drained

2 tablespoons chopped fresh flat-leaf parsley

250 g/8 oz. small squid, cleaned

2 tablespoons plain/all-purpose flour

granulated sugar (optional)

sea salt and freshly ground black pepper

Serves 4

Heat half the oil in a medium saucepan set over medium heat. Add the onion and cook for 4–5 minutes until tender but not coloured. Add the garlic, cumin, chillies/chiles and oregano and continue to cook for another minute. Add the chorizo and cook until lightly browned and the onions have started to caramelize.

Add the chopped tomatoes and beans and simmer for about 20 minutes, or until thick. Add the parsley and season with salt and pepper, plus a pinch of sugar if needed to balance the tomatoes.

Cut the squid into 1-cm/½-inch thick rings, pat dry on paper towels and toss in seasoned flour. Heat the remaining oil in a large frying pan until smoking hot, then add half the prepared squid. Cook for 2–3 minutes until golden and cooked through. Remove from the pan and cook the remaining squid. Spoon the calamari on top of the chorizo and butter/lima-bean mixture and serve immediately.

marinated anchovies

People tend to be intimidated by these little fish, but have no fear, they are easy to prepare and taste simply divine.

150 g/5½ oz. fresh anchovies
100 ml/scant ½ cup white wine vinegar
3 garlic cloves, sliced
1 tablespoon chopped fresh flat-leaf parsley
100 ml/scant ½ cup olive oil

Serves 4

To clean the anchovies, run your finger down the belly side and open up the fish. Pull the spine from the head and separate it from the flesh. Remove the head. Wash the fish and let dry on paper towels.

Put the anchovies in a plastic container and pour in the vinegar. Let them marinate in the refrigerator overnight.

Rinse the anchovies and put in a serving dish with the garlic, parsley and oil, cover and chill overnight in the refrigerator. Return to room temperature before serving with a selection of tapas. Or keep them refrigerated to eat another day – they only get better with time.

chorizo and olives in red wine
with Padrón peppers

Chorizo and olives are perfectly complemented by these small, strongly flavoured Padrón peppers. They can usually be found in good delis, but green bell peppers can also be used if they are not available.

150 g/5 oz. cooking chorizo
1 garlic clove, peeled and smashed
leaves from a sprig of fresh thyme
150 ml/⅔ cup red wine
1 tablespoon sherry vinegar or balsamic vinegar
2 tablespoons mixed olives in olive oil, plus 1 tablespoon oil from the jar

1 tablespoon chopped fresh flat-leaf parsley
150 g/5 oz. whole Padrón peppers, or sliced green bell peppers
coarse sea salt

Serves 4

Cut the chorizo into bite-size chunks. Heat a frying pan over medium heat, add the chorizo and cook until it starts to brown and crisp at the edges. Add the garlic, thyme and red wine and continue to cook until the wine has reduced by half. Add the vinegar and cook for 30 seconds then add the olives and chopped parsley.

Meanwhile, heat the tablespoon of olive oil from the jar of olives in another pan and add the whole Padrón peppers. Cook over medium heat until hot and starting to brown at the edges. Season with salt flakes and serve with the chorizo.

garlic olive oil, warm marinated olives and Serrano ham platter

This sharing plate is simplicity itself to put together and absolutely no preparation is needed once your guests arrive. Lay out the platter and let it sit at room temperature for a short while before serving.

candied salted almonds

These sweet and salty almonds make a delicious snack to serve with drinks. Once you try them, you'll be hooked! They are also great sprinkled over salads.

270 g/scant 2 cups raw almonds, unpeeled
60 g/¼ cup packed dark brown soft sugar
60 g/¼ cup maple syrup
1 teaspoon chipotle chilli/chili powder
1 tablespoon coarse sea salt

Makes 400 g/14 oz.

Preheat the oven to 190°C (375°F) Gas 5.

Put all the ingredients except for the salt in a bowl and mix until the almonds are well coated. Spread the almonds on a non-stick baking sheet and bake in the preheated oven for 5–8 minutes. The sugars will bubble and turn a darker colour.

Remove the almonds from the oven and stir with a wooden spoon. Sprinkle with salt and set aside to cool on the baking sheet. As they cool, the sugars will harden.

When the almonds have cooled, serve at room temperature.

GARLIC OLIVE OIL
8 garlic cloves, unpeeled
60 ml/¼ cup light olive oil
60 ml/¼ cup extra virgin olive oil
2 tablespoons balsamic vinegar

WARM MARINATED OLIVES
100 g/½ cup large green olives
100 g/½ cup small black olives
250 ml/1 cup extra virgin olive oil
2 sprigs of fresh thyme
2 fresh red chillies/chiles
1 bay leaf
2 thin slices of pared orange zest

TO SERVE
8 slices of Serrano ham
crusty bread

Serves 6–8

To make the garlic olive oil, put the garlic cloves and light olive oil in a small saucepan and cook over medium heat for 5 minutes. Remove from the heat and let cool. Add the extra virgin olive oil and vinegar and transfer to a serving bowl.

Put the olives in a small, heatproof bowl. Put the oil, thyme, chillies/chiles, bay leaf and orange zest in a small saucepan set over medium heat. As soon as you hear the herbs starting to sizzle in the oil, remove the pan from the heat and pour the mixture over the olives. Let cool for 20 minutes.

Arrange the warm garlic oil, olives, Serrano ham and bread on a serving platter and serve immediately.

FRENCH HORS D'OEUVRES

These are a selection of delicious cold appetizers served before a larger meal, often as a buffet. With some clever shopping and a few simple recipes, you can put together a spread of tasty French treats that makes an indulgent and satisfying meal. Hors D'oeuvres often consist of regional French cheeses, cured meats, sausages, pâtés, terrines, fresh salads and occasionally a few warm dishes and are perfect for sharing. They are always accompanied by fresh bread so a visit to a good bakery is a must. Lay out your foods artfully on wooden chopping boards and wicker trays to create a rustic feel. Serve with regional French wines such as white Burgundy or with small glasses of aniseed-flavoured Pernod.

baby asparagus
with vinaigrette and chopped egg

The freshness of the baby asparagus in this recipe is beautiful with the sharp tang of the mustardy vinaigrette.

2 bunches baby asparagus, trimmed
3 tablespoons extra virgin olive oil
1 tablespoon red wine vinegar
½ teaspoon Dijon mustard
1 shallot, finely diced
1 hard-boiled/hard-cooked egg
2 tablespoons chopped fresh flat-leaf parsley
sea salt and freshly ground black pepper

Serves 4–6

Blanch the asparagus for 2–3 minutes in a saucepan of salted boiling water. Drain and refresh in cold water. Pat dry and arrange in a serving dish.

To make the dressing, put the oil, vinegar, mustard and shallot in a small bowl and season with salt and pepper. Whisk with a fork to combine and pour it over the asparagus. Chop the egg and sprinkle it on top of the asparagus, followed by the parsley. Serve immediately.

quick mini pissaladières

These mini puff-pastry tarts hail from the south of France and have all the flavours of Provence.

275 g/9¾ oz. puff pastry sheets
5 tablespoons olive oil
750 g/1 lb 10 oz. onions, thinly sliced
3 garlic cloves, finely chopped
1 tablespoon sugar
1 tablespoon white wine vinegar
50 g/1¾ oz. anchovy fillets, halved lengthways

1 tablespoon dried herbes de provence
a handful of black olives, pitted
sea salt and freshly ground black pepper

a pastry cutter, 5–6 cm/2–3 inches in diameter

Makes 20

Preheat the oven to 200ºC (400ºF) Gas 6. Unroll the pastry sheets and use a pastry cutter to stamp out 20 circles. Refrigerate until needed. Heat the oil in a large saucepan set over medium–high heat. Add the onions and cook for about 10 minutes. Add the garlic, sugar and vinegar and season with salt and pepper. Reduce the heat to low and cook for about 20 minutes further, until the onions have caramelized. Remove the pan from the heat. Place the pastry circles on baking sheets and divide the onion mixture between them. Arrange the anchovies on top, sprinkle with the herbs and add a few olives. Bake in the preheated oven for 25 minutes, until crisp. Serve warm.

celeriac rémoulade

Remoulade is a popular condiment that is similar to tartare sauce. It is popular in many different countries, but the French variety is often made with mustard and combined with celeriac and makes a delicious hors d'oeuvre.

250 ml/1 cup crème fraîche or sour cream
freshly squeezed juice ½ lemon
2 tablespoons wholegrain mustard
500 g/1 lb 2 oz. (1 large) celeriac, peeled and coarsely shredded
a small handful of fresh flat-leaf parsley, finely chopped (optional)
sea salt and freshly ground black pepper

Serves 4–6

Put the crème fraîche, lemon juice and mustard in a medium bowl and season with salt and pepper. Whisk with a fork to combine. Add the shredded celeriac and mix well until the celeriac is coated with the dressing. Taste and adjust the seasoning. Sprinkle with parsley (if using) and refrigerate until ready to serve.

saffron and garlic aioli

This recipe originates from Provence in the south of France and is a glorious celebration of the region's produce. Traditionally, a selection of raw or blanched baby vegetables and hard-boiled/hard-cooked eggs are served with this rich, garlicky sauce for dipping.

This platter is ideal for entertaining a large group of guests. Arrange the vegetables on a large oval serving plate with a bowl of aioli as the centrepiece, then let your guests help themselves. Serve with plenty of crusty bread.

2 egg yolks, at room temperature
1 teaspoon Dijon mustard
1 teaspoon crushed saffron threads, soaked in 1 tablespoon lukewarm water
1 garlic clove, crushed
½ teaspoon each sea salt and freshly ground black pepper
200 ml/⅔ cup grapeseed or sunflower oil
1 tablespoon freshly squeezed lemon juice

TO SERVE
baby carrots with tops left on
radishes with stems and leaves left on
cucumber, sliced into thick batons
spring onions/scallions, trimmed
fennel, quartered and sliced
celery hearts with leaves left on
mangetout/snow peas
green beans, blanched
cherry tomatoes on the vine
red or yellow bell peppers, cut into strips
organic eggs, hard-boiled/hard-cooked and halved
a large loaf of good French country bread

Makes 300 ml/1⅓ cups

Put the egg yolks in a bowl or food processor and add the mustard, saffron, garlic, and salt and pepper. While whisking, slowly drizzle in the oil until incorporated. Add the lemon juice and mix again. Pour into a serving bowl and place on a platter with the eggs and vegetables. Serve immediately with slices of crusty French bread.

tapenade

Black, glossy tapenade gets its name from tapeña, the Provençal word for 'caper'. This essential ingredient, along with salted anchovies, garlic, herbs, olive oil and lemon juice, creates a heady mix. Use tapenade on toast, and eat with hard-boiled/hard-cooked egg halves or with fresh vegetables such as raw carrot, celery, fennel, cucumber and tomato. It also makes a good sauce for poached fish or grilled steaks.

350 g/2 cups black olives

100 g/¼ cup capers in brine, rinsed

6 fresh salted anchovies, boned, rinsed and chopped, or 12 canned anchovy fillets, chopped

50 g/2 oz. canned tuna in brine, drained and flaked (optional)

2–4 garlic cloves, crushed plus 1 whole garlic clove, peeled

1 teaspoon mixed dried herbs, including thyme, oregano, lavender and savory

½ teaspoon coarse sea salt

freshly ground black pepper

125 ml/½ cup extra virgin olive oil

1 tablespoon marc de Provence (eau de vie)

freshly squeezed juice of ¼ lemon (optional)

8–12 slices of baguette

rocket/arugula leaves, to serve

Serves 4–6

Put the olives in a food processor with the capers, anchovies and tuna and blend to a coarse purée.

Put the garlic, herbs, salt and pepper in a large mortar and pound with a pestle to create a pungent paste. Gradually add to the olive pulp, then process in bursts, with the oil, until creamy.

Taste and add the marc and the lemon juice, if using.

Preheat the grill/broiler to medium–hot and grill/broil the baguette slices until toasted and golden. Rub the whole garlic clove all over the toasted baguette slices.

Drizzle the tapenade over the garlicky toasts and top with rocket/arugula leaves. Serve immediately.

stuffed baby vegetables

4 medium mushrooms, with stems

4 medium tomatoes or 4 large plum tomatoes

2 courgettes/zucchini or small squash

4 Swiss chard/collard stems

2 large globe artichokes or 4 small ones

1 lemon, halved

STUFFING

4 tablespoons extra virgin olive oil, plus extra for drizzling

25 g/1 oz. stale bread, crumbled or diced

2 garlic cloves, chopped

1 onion, finely chopped

a handful of leaves from a variety of mixed fresh herbs, such as dill or marjoram, chives, parsley, borage and basil, chopped

8 allspice berries

12 black peppercorns

12 coriander seeds

½–1 teaspoon coarse sea salt

75 g/3 oz. cooked chicken or ham, chopped

100 g/½ cup cooked bacon lardons

Serves 4

Stuffing vegetables transforms them. Use plenty of fresh herbs, not dried ones.

Preheat the oven to 180°C (350°F) Gas 4. Hollow out the mushrooms, tomatoes and courgettes/zucchini, reserving the flesh and trimmings. Keep the tops of the vegetables to use as as lids. Quarter the chard/collard stems and put the vegetables in a large roasting pan.

Discard the artichoke stems and two layers of the outer leaves. Cut the remaining leaves down to 5 cm/2 inches from the base. Dig out the fluffy choke and yellow inner leaves.

Discard both. Blanch in boiling water for 2–3 minutes, then drain.

Heat the oil in a frying pan, add the breadcrumbs, garlic and onion and cook over high heat for 3 minutes, stirring often. Chop the reserved vegetable trimmings, add to the pan and cook for 10 minutes more. Add the fresh herbs.

Grind the allspice, peppercorns and coriander seeds with the salt. Combine with the breadcrumb mixture. Taste and adjust the seasoning. Fill the hollowed-out vegetables and replace the lids. Drizzle generously with olive oil and bake in the preheated oven for 25 minutes. Serve hot.

Preheat the oven to 180°C (350°F) Gas 4. Lay some of the bacon across the width of the prepared terrine, reserving some for the top.

Heat 1 tablespoon of the olive oil in a frying pan over high heat and cook the chicken livers for 1 minute until just coloured. Remove from the pan, coarsely chop and set aside. Reduce the heat to low and add the remaining oil. Sauté the onion and garlic for 10 minutes until soft but not yet browned. Put the onion, garlic, livers and all the remaining ingredients, except the bay or sage leaves, in a large bowl and mix until combined.

Put the mixture into the terrine and press down firmly. Fold over any overhanging bacon, cover with the reserved bacon and finish with the bay leaves. Cover firmly with the terrine lid or a sheet of oiled aluminium foil and place in a baking dish. Fill the baking dish with enough water to come halfway up the sides of the terrine. Bake in the oven for 75 minutes.

Remove the terrine from the oven and put it in a dish to catch any juices. Put a weight over the top, leave to cool, then refrigerate overnight or for up to 2 days. Serve with radishes and crusty bread.

farmhouse terrine

It's hard to beat a classic, rustic farmhouse terrine, full of your favourite French flavours. Traditionally, it would have included lard to give a much softer loaf, but this version is healthier, lighter and packed with flavour.

200 g/7 oz. bacon slices
3 tablespoons olive oil
250 g/9 oz. chicken livers, cleaned and trimmed
1 small onion, chopped
2 garlic cloves, finely chopped
500 g/1 lb 2 oz. pork belly, coarsely minced/ground
250 g/9 oz. veal or chicken, minced/ground
20 g/scant 1 oz. fresh breadcrumbs
8 tablespoons chopped fresh flat-leaf parsley
1 tablespoon chopped fresh thyme

1 tablespoon chopped fresh oregano
½ teaspoon ground nutmeg
½ teaspoon ground allspice
1 teaspoon sea salt
½ teaspoon freshly ground black pepper
60 ml/¼ cup brandy
125 ml/½ cup chicken stock
6 bay or sage leaves
radishes and crusty bread, to serve

a 1-litre/1-quart terrine or 25-cm/10-inch loaf pan, oiled with rapeseed oil

Serves 10–12

ham and chicken pots *with cornichons*

These little potted meats are somewhere between a pâté and a terrine. Whole green peppercorns add a real kick, but if you like a mild flavour, use mustard instead. Present them in any individual-sized pots.

300 g/10½ oz. chicken breasts, skin on

1 onion, thickly sliced

½ teaspoon black peppercorns

½ teaspoon sea salt

500 ml/2 cups chicken stock

3 sheets of leaf gelatine or 1 tablespoon powdered gelatine

60 ml/¼ cup dry white wine

300 g/10½ oz. thickly sliced ham

4 tablespoons chopped fresh flat-leaf parsley

1 tablespoon green peppercorns in brine, drained, or wholegrain mustard

slices of crusty bread, and cornichons, to serve

6 ramekins

Serves 6

Put the chicken breasts in a saucepan with the onion, black peppercorns and salt. Add the chicken stock. Bring to the boil, then reduce to a low simmer. Cook, partially covered, for 15–20 minutes, until the chicken is cooked through. Remove from the heat, cover tightly and leave off the heat to continue cooking for a further 20 minutes. Remove the chicken from the stock (reserving the stock), leave to cool and discard the skin, then cut the meat into small dice.

Drain 300 ml/1¼ cups of the hot stock into a large jug. Put the leaf gelatine sheets (if using), one at a time, in cold water. Leave for

1 minute, then remove and squeeze out any excess water. Add the gelatine (or powdered gelatine, if using) to the hot stock and stir to dissolve. Stir in the wine.

Put the ham in a food processor and process in bursts until finely chopped.

In a bowl, combine the chicken, ham, parsley and green peppercorns. Divide the mixture between the ramekins. Pour over the gelatinous stock. Refrigerate for 3–4 hours until set. Serve with crusty bread and cornichons.

salads & summer soups

Catalan salad *with tuna and aioli*

This Catalan salad is a refreshing change from the more usual salade Niçoise. The Serrano ham makes for an altogether more savoury dish and the formal arrangement of the ingredients on a platter, as opposed to being chopped up in a salad bowl, looks stunning. Aioli is a Catalan favourite and is also delicious served with raw or cooked vegetables.

100 g/⅔ cup green beans
2 baby romaine lettuces
100 g/3½ oz. thinly sliced Serrano ham
4 hard-boiled/hard-cooked eggs, halved
200 g/⅔ cup canned tuna, drained and broken into large chunks
8 large pitted green olives, halved
2 tablespoons extra virgin olive oil
2 tablespoons sherry or red wine vinegar
sea salt and freshly ground black pepper

AIOLI
4 garlic cloves, unpeeled
½ teaspoon sea salt
2 teaspoons freshly squeezed lemon juice
1 egg yolk
175 ml/⅔ cup extra virgin olive oil

Serves 4

To make the aioli, put the garlic cloves in a mortar and bash them lightly with a pestle, pulling away the skin as it frees itself. Add the salt and grind the garlic to a smooth paste. Transfer to a large, wide bowl, add the lemon juice and the egg yolk and whisk with a metal whisk. Continue whisking as you add the olive oil a few drops at a time; as the aioli starts to thicken, add the oil in a slow, steady stream. This should take about 5 minutes. If you prefer a lighter mayonnaise, whisk in 2 tablespoons of boiling water. Transfer to a serving bowl, cover and chill until required.

Cook the beans in salted boiling water for 7–10 minutes until al dente, then drain and refresh in iced water. Drain and dry. Cover a large platter with lettuce leaves, then fan the beans around the rim of the platter, sticking out from under the edge of the lettuce leaves. Twist the slices of Serrano ham and arrange them on the lettuce leaves, then arrange the eggs, tuna and olive halves on top. Drizzle the olive oil and vinegar over the salad, then season with salt and pepper. Serve immediately with the aioli in a separate bowl.

summer leaf and herb salad

There are thousands of recipes for simple leaf salads, but the combination of lovely fresh herbs with a varied mixture of salad leaves and a tangy lemon dressing is always a winner.

inner leaves from 2 large cos lettuces

250 g/3⅓ cups mixed salad leaves, such as radicchio, mâche, lamb's lettuce/corn salad, mizuna or chicory

a handful of fresh mixed herbs such as basil, chives, dill and mint

HONEY LEMON DRESSING

1 garlic clove, crushed

125 ml/½ cup extra virgin olive oil

1 tablespoon lemon juice

1 teaspoon clear honey

1 teaspoon Dijon mustard

sea salt and freshly ground black pepper

Serves 4

Put the dressing ingredients into a bowl or small jug and set aside to infuse for at least 1 hour. Just before serving, strain out the garlic.

Wash the leaves, pat dry with paper towels and transfer to a plastic bag. Chill for 30 minutes to make the leaves crisp.

Put the leaves and herbs into a serving bowl, add a little of the dressing and toss well to coat evenly. Add a little more dressing to taste, then serve.

tomato salad *with anchovy vinaigrette*

Anchoïade is a Provençal anchovy sauce/dip, which is spread thickly on grilled bread slices, or served with raw vegetables as a starter. Here it has been adpated to become a dressing for ripe, flavourful vine tomatoes. If these are not available, use boiled baby new potatoes instead and toss while the potatoes are still warm. Serve as an accompaniment to griled fish or meat.

To make the vinaigrette, put the garlic, mustard, vinegar and anchovies in a food processor and blend to a purée. Add the oil, 1 tablespoon at a time, then blend in the basil. Season with pepper and set aside.

Cut the tomatoes into quarters or eighths, depending on their size. Arrange on a plate and sprinkle with the shallot. Season lightly with salt, then spoon the dressing over the top. Sprinkle with the parsley, basil and some pepper and serve at room temperature.

750 g/1 lb 10 oz. ripe vine tomatoes
1 large shallot, thinly sliced
coarse sea salt and freshly ground black pepper

ANCHOVY VINAIGRETTE
1 garlic clove
½ teaspoon Dijon mustard
2 tablespoons white wine vinegar
6 anchovy fillets in oil
8 tablespoons extra virgin olive oil
a small handful of basil leaves
freshly ground black pepper

TO SERVE
a handful of fresh flat-leaf parsley, finely chopped
a few basil leaves, torn

Serves 4

chicory salad *with Roquefort, celery and walnuts*

Developed unintentionally by a gardener at the Brussels botanical gardens in the middle of the nineteenth century, chicory is now cultivated for a good part of the year, and modern varieties have none of the bitterness of their ancestors. When buying, choose very pale chicory with only a hint of green; they grow in the dark, so colour on the leaves is a sign that they have been exposed to the light and are not as fresh. Also, bigger is not necessarily better; 20 cm/8 inches is the maximum length for best taste.

4–5 heads of chicory, halved, cored and thinly sliced

2 celery stalks, thinly sliced, plus a few leaves, torn

70 g/2½ oz. Roquefort cheese, crumbled

50 g/½ cup shelled walnuts, chopped

a handful of fresh flat-leaf parsley, chopped

1 baguette, sliced, to serve

WALNUT VINAIGRETTE

2 tablespoons white wine vinegar

1 teaspoon sea salt

1 teaspoon Dijon mustard

7 tablespoons sunflower oil

1 tablespoon walnut oil (optional)

freshly ground black pepper

Serves 4

To prepare the vinaigrette, put the vinegar in a large bowl. Using a fork or a small whisk, stir in the salt until almost dissolved. You may have to tilt the bowl so the vinegar is deep enough to have something to stir. Mix in the mustard until completely blended. Add the sunflower oil, a tablespoon at a time, beating well between each addition, until emulsified. Add the walnut oil, and, if using, use one less tablespoon of sunflower oil. Season with pepper to taste.

Add the chicory, celery, Roquefort, walnuts and parsley and toss well to coat with the dressing. Serve immediately with slices of crusty baguette.

spicy pasta salad
with tuna and feta

Canned tuna works so well with the simple, fresh Mediterranean flavours in this salad, such as lemon and parsley. The inclusion of feta cheese here may seem a little odd, but it really does work. Just a small amount provides an extra tangy, savoury element to this summery dish. Any large, open pasta shape will work, but lumaconi have been used here, which translates as 'big snail shells' in Italian.

400 g/14 oz. large dried pasta shapes,
such as lumaconi
65 ml/¼ cup olive oil
2 red onions, finely chopped
2 garlic cloves, finely chopped
1 large red chilli/chile, deseeded and finely chopped
2 tablespoons small capers in brine, rinsed
1 tablespoon red wine vinegar
400-g/14-oz. can tuna in oil, drained
50 g/1¾ oz. feta cheese, crumbled
50 g/scant 1 cup wild rocket/arugula
sea salt and freshly ground black pepper
lemon wedges, to serve

Serves 4

Bring a large saucepan of lightly salted water to the boil. Add the pasta and cook for 8–10 minutes, until tender. Drain well and add 1 tablespoon of the olive oil. Transfer to a large bowl.

Heat the remaining oil in a large frying pan set over high heat. Add the onions, garlic, chilli/chile and capers and cook for 2–3 minutes, stirring frequently until the onion has softened. Add the vinegar and cook for 1 minute further. Add the tuna and use a fork to roughly break up any larger chunks.

Add the tuna mixture to the bowl with the pasta. Add the feta and rocket/arugula and toss to combine. Season with salt and pepper to taste. Serve warm or cold with lemon wedges for squeezing.

grilled mixed vegetable salad *with balsamic herb dressing*

This is one of the easiest ways to cook and serve a selection of Mediterranean vegetables for a large number of people. Grilling/broiling the vegetables concentrates their flavours, and a touch of aged balsamic vinegar cuts through their sweetness. Don't cut the vegetables too small – this salad should be robust and chunky.

1 medium courgette/zucchini
1 medium aubergine/eggplant
1 large red bell pepper, halved
12 tablespoons extra virgin olive oil
2 small red onions, quartered
150 g/⅔ cup cherry tomatoes
2 teaspoons balsamic vinegar
1 garlic clove, crushed
3 tablespoons chopped mixed fresh herbs, such as parsley, basil, marjoram or oregano, plus extra to serve
sea salt and freshly ground black pepper

Serves 4

Cut the courgette/zucchini, aubergine/eggplant and the pepper into large, bite-sized pieces. Transfer to a large bowl, add 6 tablespoons olive oil and toss well to coat. Season with salt and pepper to taste.

Line a grill/broiler pan with foil and spoon in the vegetables. Add the onions and spread out the vegetables in an even layer (don't overcrowd the pan or they will stew). Grill/broil for 4–5 minutes. Stir well, add the tomatoes and grill for a further 5 minutes until the vegetables are browned and cooked but not mushy.

Meanwhile, whisk the remaining olive oil with the balsamic vinegar, garlic and herbs. Pour the dressing over the vegetables, toss lightly and transfer to a serving dish. Cover and set aside for at least 30 minutes to let the flavours infuse. Sprinkle with extra herbs and serve warm or at room temperature.

insalata Nizzarda

This is one of the few Mediterranean salads popular throughout Italy that is served as a main meal. It originates in Nice (Nizza), which was a part of Italy until 1861. It has many local variations, which means the selection of vegetables may vary, but the constants are tomatoes, eggs, olives, tuna and anchovies.

Put the oil, vinegar, garlic and basil in a bowl and whisk. Season well with salt and pepper.

Cut the tomatoes into sixths and put in a large bowl. Add the peppers, cucumber, onion, celery, artichokes, olives and radishes. Spoon over half the dressing and toss well to coat. Pile onto a large serving platter. Add the tuna to the salad and arrange the eggs and anchovies on top. Spoon over the remaining dressing, sprinkle with basil leaves and serve immediately.

8 tablespoons extra virgin olive oil

3 tablespoons vinegar

2 garlic cloves, crushed

3 tablespoons chopped fresh basil leaves, plus extra to serve

3 ripe tomatoes

2 green or yellow bell peppers, sliced

1 cucumber, cut into chunks

1 red onion, finely chopped

1 celery stalk, sliced

500 g/1 lb 2 oz. grilled artichokes in oil, drained and halved

50 g/scant ⅓ cup mixed black and green olives

5–6 radishes, trimmed

250 g/9 oz. canned tuna in oil, drained and broken into chunks

3 hard-boiled/hard-cooked eggs, quartered

12 anchovy fillets in oil, drained

sea salt and freshly ground black pepper

Serves 6

seafood salad
with lemon and parsley

Versions of this type of salad are found all along the coastal regions of Italy. Use only the freshest seafood, clean it really well and cook it quickly. Use as much lemon as you like to bring out the flavour of the seafood and cut through its richness. Scallops and baby octopus are good additions.

500 g/1 lb 2 oz. fresh mussels, in their shells

1.5 kg/3 lb 5 oz. fresh vongole or other small clams, in their shells

250 g/9 oz. small fresh squid, cleaned, tentacles removed and bodies cut into rings

250 g/9 oz. small raw prawns/shrimp, in their shells

6 tablespoons extra virgin olive oil

finely grated zest and juice of 1 lemon

1 garlic clove, finely chopped

4 tablespoons chopped fresh flat-leaf parsley

1 lettuce, leaves separated

sea salt and freshly ground black pepper

lemon wedges, to serve

Serves 4

Debeard the mussels. Scrub the mussels and clams, discarding any with damaged shells or ones that don't close when sharply tapped. Put them in a large bowl of cold water to purge for about 15 minutes. Drain them and put in a large saucepan. Place the pan over high heat, cover and cook for about 5 minutes, shaking the pan occasionally, until the shells open (discard any that don't open). Tip into a colander placed over a saucepan to catch the juices. Remove the clam and mussel meat from the shells.

Bring the reserved juices to the boil and add the squid and prawns/shrimp. Cook for 2–3 minutes until cooked through, then drain. Peel the prawns/shrimp then put them in a bowl with the squid and clam and mussel meat and mix well.

Put the oil, lemon zest and juice, parsley and garlic in a bowl. Season with salt and pepper and whisk. Pour over the seafood and mix well. Cover and refrigerate for at least 1 hour. Arrange the lettuce leaves on a serving platter and top with the seafood. Serve immediately with lemon wedges for squeezing.

Greek barley salad

This hearty version of the traditional Greek salad incorporates satisfying barley and lots of fresh vegetables. If you are able to buy good-quality dried Greek oregano, it will make all the difference to the flavour.

100 g/½ cup pearl barley

freshly squeezed juice and finely grated zest of 1 lemon

2 teaspoons white or red wine vinegar

4 tablespoons extra virgin olive oil

1 red onion, thinly sliced

4 tomatoes, chopped

1 large cucumber or 2 small, deseeded and chopped

1 green bell pepper, chopped

20 kalamata olives

150 g/5½ oz. feta cheese

1 teaspoon dried oregano

sea salt and freshly ground black pepper

Serves 4

Cook the barley in a saucepan of boiling salted water for 30 minutes or until tender. Drain and set aside until needed.

In a large serving bowl, whisk together the lemon juice and zest, vinegar and oil, then stir in the warm barley and mix well. Let cool.

Soak the onion in a bowl of iced water for 10 minutes. Drain well.

Add the drained onion to the barley along with the tomatoes, cucumber, green pepper and olives and mix to combine. Season with salt and pepper to taste.

Crumble the feta over the top of the salad and sprinkle with oregano. Serve immediately.

tuna and cannellini bean salad

This uncomplicated salad makes a filling meal served with fresh bread. As it features two canned ingredients, you can usually whip it up at short notice. If you have tuna in good-quality olive oil, use the oil in the salad.

1 red onion, thinly sliced

185 g/⅔ cup canned tuna in oil, drained

400-g/14-oz. can cannellini beans, drained and rinsed

a large bunch of flat-leaf parsley, chopped

freshly squeezed juice of 1 lemon

4 tablespoons extra virgin olive oil

sea salt and freshly ground black pepper

fresh bread, to serve

Serves 2-3

orange, endive and black olive salad

In Sicily, the land of orange and lemon groves, this salad is often served after grilled fish – especially in the region around Palermo. It is another example of their passion for sweet and savoury combinations and is very refreshing.

To make the dressing, put the orange zest and juice, olive oil, basil, olives and sun-dried tomatoes in a large bowl. Mix well, season with salt and pepper and set aside to develop the flavours.

Peel the oranges with a sharp knife, removing all the skin and white pith. Cut out the segments. Set aside in a bowl. Finely slice the onion, using a very sharp thin-bladed knife or a Japanese mandolin. Immediately toss the onion and oranges in the dressing to prevent discoloration. Let marinate in a cool place for 15 minutes.

Put the escarole on a plate and pile the dressed orange and onion mixture in the centre, spooning over any remaining dressing. Serve immediately.

2 oranges
1 red onion
125 g/scant 2 cups escarole, curly endive or frisée

DRESSING
finely grated zest and juice of 1 orange
6 tablespoons extra virgin olive oil
2 tablespoons chopped fresh basil
2 tablespoons finely chopped, pitted, Greek-style, oven-dried black olives
2 sun-dried tomatoes in oil, finely chopped
sea salt and freshly ground black pepper

Serves 4

Soak the onion slices in iced water for 10 minutes. Drain well.

Put the onion, tuna, cannellini beans and parsley in a large serving bowl. Add the lemon juice and oil and toss gently to combine.

Season to taste with salt and pepper. Serve with plenty of fresh bread.

avocado and chickpea salad

2 eggs

250 g/3½ cups baby spinach

400-g/14-oz. can chickpeas, rinsed
and drained

2 ripe avocados, halved, pitted,
peeled and sliced

2 teaspoons pimentón dulce
(Spanish sweet paprika)

CREAMY CHIVE DRESSING

freshly squeezed juice of 1 lemon

3 tablespoons milk

2 tablespoons plain yogurt

a bunch of chives, chopped

sea salt and freshly ground
black pepper

Serves 4

This is a fresh and yet instant meal for lazy evenings. When buying avocados, make sure that they are slightly soft to the touch and blemish-free.

Put the eggs in a small saucepan of water, bring to the boil and cook for 8–9 minutes until hard-boiled/hard-cooked. Drain, cool, shell, cut into quarters and set aside.

To make the dressing, put the lemon juice in a bowl with the milk, yogurt and chopped chives. Season generously with salt and pepper and stir until smooth.

Put the spinach, chickpeas, avocados and eggs in a bowl and sprinkle with the paprika. Spoon over the dressing and serve immediately.

watermelon and ricotta salata salad *with olive salt*

This is a delightfully pretty and refreshing salad in which the olive salt brings out the sweetness of the watermelon. Ricotta salata, a lightly salted cheese made from sheep's milk, originates from the island of Sicily. If you can't find a mini watermelon, buy the smallest available and cut it in half. You can use feta cheese if ricotta salata isn't available.

1 mini seedless watermelon
170 g/⅔ cup ricotta salata cheese
2 tablespoons fresh oregano leaves
olive oil, for drizzling
freshly ground black pepper

OLIVE SALT
10 black olives, pitted
2½ tablespoons sea salt

Serves 2

Peel the watermelon and cut it into bite-sized chunks. Put in a serving bowl, crumble the ricotta salata over the watermelon and sprinkle with the oregano.

To make the olive salt, chop the olives roughly. Grind them with the salt using a pestle and mortar until the olives are mashed.

Drizzle the olive oil over the salad and season with black pepper. Sprinkle with olive salt to taste and serve immediately.

heirloom tomato, burrata and basil summer salad

A deluxe version of the eternally popular tomato and mozzarella salad using burrata, a wonderful fresh cheese from Puglia which is based on mozzarella and cream. A real high summer treat.

Remove the stalks from the tomatoes. Slice the larger ones and halve the smaller ones or leave them whole. Transfer to a bowl. Spoon over the olive oil, season with salt and pepper, toss well to coat and leave for 10 minutes.

Divide the tomatoes between 4 small plates. Roughly tear the Burrata into small chunks and distribute them over the tomatoes. Scatter with the basil leaves. Drizzle over a little more oil and some balsamic vinegar, and serve immediately.

400 g/14 oz. mixed heirloom tomatoes in different colours
3–4 tablespoons extra virgin olive oil, plus extra for drizzling
300 g/10½ oz. burrata cheese
leaves from 3 sprigs of fresh basil (purple basil, if possible)
balsamic vinegar, for drizzling
sea salt and freshly ground black pepper

Serves 4

feta, cucumber and mint spring salad

A fabulously fresh-tasting summery salad with bright flavours of cucumber and radish combined with the salty tang of feta cheese and olives. Perfect for eating alfresco.

2 mini cucumbers
6 breakfast radishes
2 good handfuls of rocket/arugula
a small handful of fresh mint leaves
150 g/5½ oz. feta cheese, crumbled
10–15 small black olives

DRESSING
3 tablespoons extra virgin olive oil
1 tablespoon red wine vinegar
a good squeeze of lemon juice
sea salt and freshly ground black pepper

Serves 2

To make the dressing, put the olive oil, vinegar, lemon juice and pepper in a bowl and whisk to blend.

Cut the cucumbers in half lengthways and scoop out the seeds with the tip of a teaspoon. Slice lengthways using a vegetable peeler to make wafer-thin slices. Trim the radishes and thinly slice on the diagonal.

Put the rocket/arugula, mint, cucumber and radishes in a serving bowl. Add the dressing and toss well to coat. Add the crumbled feta and toss lightly again, then scatter over the olives. Serve immediately.

ajo blanco

Similar to gazpacho, this cold soup hailing from Malaga, Spain, makes a refreshing summer appetizer or light lunch. It is worth taking the time to chill the soup for an hour or so to let the flavours develop.

2 thick slices of stale white country-style bread, crusts removed
3 garlic cloves, peeled
150 g/1 cup blanched almonds, very finely ground
150 ml/scant ⅔ cup extra virgin olive oil
2 tablespoons sherry vinegar (or to taste)
a small bunch of white grapes, halved
salt and black pepper

Serves 2–4

Soak the bread in a little water for 5 minutes or so to soften it. Squeeze out the excess water and transfer the bread to a food processor. Add the garlic, ground almonds and 800 ml/ 3 cups water and blend until smooth. Season to taste. If possible, refrigerate the soup for an hour or so to allow the lovely garlicky flavour to develop.

Stir in 100 ml/scant ½ cup of the olive oil and the sherry vinegar. Taste and adjust the seasoning and spoon into chilled bowls. Drizzle over the remaining olive oil and garnish with white grapes. Serve immediately.

soupe verdon

This bright green soup is named after the beautiful river in Provence, north of Brignoles where the green minerals in the rocky bed make the water a wonderful colour. It can be served hot or cold – you will get maximum colour, flavour and goodness if you blend the herbs into the chilled soup.

1 tablespoon sunflower oil
1 large onion, finely chopped
100 g/3½ oz. potato, diced
1 apple, peeled and finely chopped
850 ml/scant 3½ cups chicken or vegetable stock
a large bunch of watercress
a handful of fresh chervil
salt and black pepper

TO SERVE
double/heavy cream or crème fraîche
avruga or other caviar (optional)

Serves 4–6

Heat the oil and onion in a saucepan set over low heat then cook for 5 minutes until softened. Add the potato and apple, cover and cook 5 minutes further. Add the stock and bring to the boil, lower the heat and simmer for 10 minutes. Season with salt and pepper.

Remove any tough stalks from the watercress and remove the chervil stalks. Chop the watercress and chervil leaves and add to the soup. Simmer for 1 minute, then strain through a sieve/strainer into a clean pan. Put the solids from the sieve/strainer into a blender with a little of the liquid and process to a purée. Return to the pan and reheat gently then serve with a swirl of cream or crème fraîche and a spoonful of caviar, if using.

vegetable bouillabaisse

Here's a very good vegetable-only alternative to the usual tasty bouillabaisse that has fish and shellfish as a base. It has all the same flavours, including the best part – the spicy rouille sauce.

4 tablespoons olive oil
2 leeks, chopped
1 large onion, coarsely chopped
1 fennel bulb, chopped
3 garlic cloves, crushed
3 large ripe tomatoes, skinned, deseeded and chopped
5 new potatoes, chopped
2 litres/8 cups vegetable stock
1 bay leaf
a sprig of fresh thyme
a strip of peel from 1 orange
1 teaspoon saffron strands
1 baguette, sliced, for croutons
100 g/3½ oz. Gruyère cheese, grated
sea salt and freshly ground black pepper
chopped fresh flat-leaf parsley, to serve

ROUILLE
3 garlic cloves, finely chopped
1–2 fresh red chillies/chiles, finely chopped
1 egg yolk, at room temperature
300 ml/1½ cups olive oil

Serves 4–6

Heat the oil in a large saucepan set over medium heat. Add the leeks, onion and fennel and cook for 10 minutes or until just beginning to brown. Stir in the garlic, tomatoes, potatoes and 1 teaspoon salt and cook for 1 minute. Add the stock, bay leaf, thyme, orange peel and saffron and stir. Bring to the boil, reduce the heat and simmer gently for about 40 minutes until the potatoes are tender. Season to taste, cover and let stand for at least 1 hour, or cool and refrigerate overnight.

Preheat the oven to 180°C (350°F) Gas 4.

Before serving, make the croutons. Arrange the baguette slices in a single layer on a baking sheet. Bake in the preheated oven for 5–8 minutes until golden. Set aside.

To make the rouille, put the garlic, chillies/chiles and egg yolk in a small, deep bowl and whisk well to blend. Add the oil bit by bit and whisk vigorously, until the mixture is thick like mayonnaise.

To serve, warm the soup if necessary. Put 2–3 croutons in each serving bowl, sprinkle with the grated cheese and ladle in the soup. Sprinkle with chopped parsley and stir in the rouille. Serve immediately.

creamy tomato and bread soup *with basil oil*

This soup is only as good as its ingredients - great tomatoes, good bread and wonderful olive oil. This is one of the most comforting soups on earth and it has its origins in peasant thrift. Leftover bread is never thrown away in Tuscany - there is always a use for it.

1.5 litres/6 cups chicken or vegetable stock

4 tablespoons olive oil

1 onion, chopped

1.25 kg/2 lb 12 oz. very ripe tomatoes, coarsely chopped

300 g/10½ oz. stale white bread, sliced, crusts removed 3 garlic cloves, crushed

125 g/1¼ cups finely grated Parmesan, plus extra to serve

sea salt and freshly ground black pepper

BASIL OIL (optional)

6 tablespoons freshly chopped basil

150 ml/scant ⅔ cup extra virgin olive oil

Serves 6

Heat the stock in a large saucepan set over low heat. Meanwhile, heat the oil in a second large saucepan, add the onion and tomatoes and fry over low heat for about 10 minutes until soft. Push the mixture through a sieve/strainer and stir into the hot broth, then add the bread and the

chicken avgolemono

This classic Greek recipe is great for using up leftover cooked chicken. The idea of eating soup with egg and lemon juice may sound unusual, but it works. In Greece, soup is regarded as a main meal, with family members having second or even third helpings.

1.4 litres/5½ cups chicken stock

100 g/scant ½ cup rice

400 g/14 oz. cooked chicken, shredded

3 eggs

freshly squeezed juice of 1 lemon

FRIED GARLIC CROUTONS

100 ml/scant ½ cup olive oil

3 slices of stale white bread, cut into 2-cm/¾-inch cubes

4 whole garlic cloves, unpeeled

chopped fresh flat-leaf parsley

Serves 4

To make the croutons, heat the oil in a frying pan over high heat. Add the bread and garlic. Cook, stirring constantly, over medium heat for 2 minutes, or until golden brown. Discard the garlic and drain the croutons on paper towels.

Heat the stock in a large saucepan and add the rice. Bring to the boil and simmer for 15 minutes or until the rice is tender. Add the chicken and warm through for 2–3 minutes.

In the meantime, whisk the eggs with the lemon juice in a small bowl. Add a ladleful of the warm stock and whisk until thinned. Remove the soup from the heat and gradually pour in the egg mixture, whisking to amalgamate it. It should thicken in the residual heat, but if you need to, place it over low heat for just 3–4 minutes, stirring the bottom of the pan to thicken. Do not return to high heat once the egg has been added, or it will boil and scramble.

Divide the soup between warmed serving bowls and garnish with parsley and fried garlic croutons. Serve immediately.

garlic. Cover and simmer gently for about 45 minutes until thick and creamy, whisking from time to time to break up the bread. Take care, because this soup can catch on the bottom.

Meanwhile, to make the basil oil, put the basil and olive oil in a blender and purée until completely smooth.

Stir in the Parmesan, then add salt and pepper to taste. Ladle into bowls and drizzle 2 tablespoons basil oil over each serving. Serve hot, warm or cold, topped with finely grated Parmesan.

Mediterranean fish soup

There are many delectable versions of fish soup around the Mediterranean. This recipe is from Sorrento in Italy.

Chop the fish into 5-cm/2-inch chunks or, if small, leave whole. Put in a large, heatproof casserole dish. Add the peppercorns, herbs, wine and stock. Bring to the boil, then reduce the heat to a gentle simmer and cover. Cook over low heat for 5–6 minutes.

Using a slotted spoon, remove the fish to a heatproof plate and keep warm. Measure the broth – there should be about 550 ml/2¼ cups or so – if not add extra water. Pour into a jug or bowl.

Add the oil, onion, garlic and chillies/chiles to the hot pan, fry for 2 minutes, then add the tomatoes. Return the fish and broth to the pan and heat until simmering. Divide the toasted bread between warmed serving bowls, ladle the soup over the top and serve immediately.

3 kg/6 lb 8 oz. fish and mixed seafood, such as red snapper, bream, monkfish, sea bass, squid, clams and crayfish or prawns/shrimp

20 black peppercorns

a large bunch mixed fresh herbs, such as parsley, rosemary and marjoram

300 ml/2¼ cups dry white wine

300 ml//2¼ cups fish stock or water

2 tablespoons extra virgin olive oil

1 large red onion, sliced

4 garlic cloves, sliced

2 dried red chillies/chiles, crushed

4 plum tomatoes, skinned or 450 g/2 cups canned chopped tomatoes

4–6 slices of bread, 2 cm/¾ inch thick, toasted

Serves 4–6

Provençal fish soup

50 ml/¼ cup extra virgin olive oil

4 garlic cloves, chopped

2 onions, sliced

6 tomatoes, chopped

1 large fresh bouquet garni: orange zest, parsley, thyme, celery and fennel, tied together

450 g/1 lb small rockfish or carcasses (without gills) of cod, whiting etc.

200 ml/¾ cup dry white wine

2 pinches of saffron

1 teaspoon coarse sea salt

½ teaspoon dried chilli/hot pepper flakes (optional)

FISH

1 scorpion fish or red gurnard, cut into 2-cm/¾-inch slices

a 12-cm/4½-inch piece prepared monkfish, cut into 2-cm/¾ inch slices

a 12-cm/4½-inch piece John Dory or bream, cut into 2-cm/¾-inch slices

a 12-cm/4½-inch piece red snapper, cut into 2-cm/¾-inch slices

4 small red mullet or 1 large, cut into 2-cm/¾-inch slices

2 tablespoons pastis (optional)

TO SERVE

24 ready-made croûtes, or slices of baguette, toasted

rouille (see method)

100 g/1 cup Gruyère cheese, grated

Serves 4–6

This magnificent dish, not so much a soup as an entire meal, makes a glorious centrepiece at any dinner party. The manner of serving is in stages: into each dish go several dry croûtes, a dollop of rouille (a spicy red sauce) and some Gruyère, then the broth is poured into the dish. This is enjoyed first. After that the fish itself is served.

Heat the oil in a large heavy-based saucepan or heatproof casserole dish and cook the garlic and onions over high heat for 2 minutes. Add the tomatoes, bouquet garni and the rockfish. Cook for 3 minutes further. Pour in 1.5 litres/6 cups cold water and the wine and bring back to the boil. Skim off any scum, then boil for 8–10 minutes, pressing down on the fish to extract all their flavours.

Meanwhile, using a pestle and mortar, pound together the saffron, salt and dried chilli/hot pepper flakes (if using). Stir half the mixture into the soup, turn off the heat and let stand for 5 minutes.

Ladle and/or pour the pan contents into a colander or large sieve/strainer set over a bowl. Press down hard to extract all the juices and flavours but do not mash. Discard the solids, but reserve the bouquet garni.

Return the soup to its original pan. Add the fish in the order listed in the ingredients, leaving the more delicate ones until last.

Sprinkle over the remaining saffron mixture and add the reserved bouquet garni. Bring to a gentle boil and cook for 2 minutes. Reduce the heat to a lively simmer, then part-cover and cook for 5–8 minutes more, or until all the fish is tender and very hot. Taste the liquid and adjust the seasoning, if necessary: it should be a spicy reddish broth.

Put several croûtes in each warmed serving bowl and top each with a spoonful of rouille (see below) and a sprinkle of Gruyère. To serve the broth, Ladle the broth over the top and serve immediately.

Serve the fish after the broth, offering any remaining croûtes, rouille and cheese with it.

To make the rouille, dip a 5-cm/2 inch baguette into the fish broth. Squeeze it dry. Pound it with a similar volume of Aïoli (see page 41) and 2 pinches each of dried chilli/hot pepper flakes and pimiento or 1 tablespoon of ready-made harissa (Moroccan chilli/chile paste).

minted pea soup
with frazzled prosciutto

Serve this vibrant, zingy soup chilled and in small glasses. It can be prepared and chilled in advance and garnished just before serving.

1 bunch of spring onions/scallions
1 tablespoon olive oil
1 large garlic clove, crushed
1 potato, peeled and diced
750 ml/3 cups hot vegetable stock
300 g/3½ cups frozen peas
a large handful of rocket/arugula, roughly chopped
1 generous tablespoon chopped fresh mint
sea salt and freshly ground black pepper

TO GARNISH
4 slices of prosciutto
1 tablespoon olive oil
crème fraîche or sour cream
pea shoots

4–6 small glasses

Serves 4–6

Trim and slice the spring onions/scallions. Heat the oil in a saucepan set over medium heat, add the spring onions/scallions and garlic and cook for a couple of minutes until tender but not coloured. Add the diced potato to the pan along with the vegetable stock. Bring to the boil, then simmer gently for about 20 minutes, or until the potato is really tender. Add the peas, rocket/arugula and mint and cook for a further 3–4 minutes.

Tip the contents of the pan into a food processor and blend until smooth. Pass the soup through a fine sieve/strainer and season with salt and pepper. If the soup is too thick, add a little more vegetable stock. Cover and chill the soup until ready to serve.

To garnish, roughly tear the prosciutto into pieces. Heat the oil in a frying pan, add the prosciutto and cook until crisp. Remove from the heat and drain on paper towels.

Divide the soup between 4–6 small glasses. Add a teaspoon of crème fraîche to each, top with pea shoots, crisp prosciutto and black pepper. Serve immediately.

gazpacho

There are more than thirty variations of gazpacho, only some of which are the familiar raw, cold, tomato-based mixture. This version is typical of Andalusia in the south of Spain. Originally, it was a peasant dish that made use of the three basic ingredients much revered in Spain – oil, water and bread (in Arabic, gazpacho means 'soaked bread'). Other ingredients were added according to what was available.

1 large onion, finely chopped

1½ teaspoons caster/granulated sugar

4 tablespoons white wine vinegar

1 large red bell pepper, peeled with a vegetable peeler and coarsely chopped

1 large green bell pepper, peeled with a vegetable peeler and coarsely chopped

3 slices country-style bread, with crusts, about 100 g/3½ oz.

3 garlic cloves, crushed

2.5 kg/5 lb 8 oz. ripe tomatoes, skinned

a 12-cm/4½-inch piece cucumber, peeled and coarsely chopped

6 tablespoons virgin olive oil

fine sea salt

a splash of Tabasco (optional)

ice (optional)

GARNISHES

a 6-cm/2½-inch piece cucumber, unpeeled, finely chopped

ready-made croutons

2 ripe tomatoes, finely chopped

Serves 6

Put a quarter of the chopped onion in a small bowl and add ¼ teaspoon of the sugar, ½ teaspoon vinegar and 3 tablespoons cold water and set aside. Reserve a quarter of the prepared peppers and put in small bowls. These small bowls will be served as garnishes at the end. To make the other garnishes, put the unpeeled chopped cucumber, croutons and chopped tomatoes in separate small bowls and set aside.

To make the gazpacho, put the bread, garlic and remaining sugar in a flat dish, sprinkle with the remaining vinegar and 250 ml/1 cup cold water and let soak.

Cut the skinned tomatoes in half and cut out the hard core. Put a sieve/strainer over a bowl and deseed the tomatoes into the sieve/strainer. Push the seeds with a ladle to extract all the juices. Put the juices in a food processor and discard the seeds. Add the soaked bread mixture and half the tomato flesh. Blend until smooth and pour into a bowl.

Put the remaining tomatoes, the remaining onion and 100 ml/scant ½ cup iced water in the food processor and blend to a coarse purée, then pour into the bowl. Put the remaining peppers, cucumber, oil, some salt and 150 ml/scant ⅔ cup iced water in the food processor and blend to a coarse purée. Add to the bowl and stir in the Tabasco, if using. Chill for up to 2 hours.

Divide the soup between chilled serving bowls. Serve immediately with crushed ice cubes, if liked, and the bowls of garnishes for scattering over the gazpacho.

from the grill

Cover with a double layer of plastic wrap and let marinate in the refrigerator for 24 hours, turning a couple of times. Bring to room temperature before cooking.

Preheat the barbecue to hot. Take the meat out of the marinade and remove any pieces of garlic or rosemary from the steak. Pat dry with paper towels. Cook the steak over hot coals for about 4 minutes on one side, then turn the steak over and cook for a further 3 minutes. (Cook for a couple of minutes longer on each side for a medium-rare steak, although this is traditionally served rare.)

Transfer to a warm plate and season both sides with salt and pepper. Cover lightly with aluminium foil, then let rest for 5 minutes.

Stand the steak upright with the bone at the bottom and, using a sharp knife, remove the meat either side of the bone in one piece. Cut the meat into slices and divide between 2 serving plates. Pour over any meat juices that have accumulated under the meat and drizzle with extra virgin olive oil.

Serve with sautéed potatoes, a rocket/arugula salad and lemon wedges for squeezing.

Tuscan-style steak

1 large T-bone steak, about 700 g/1 lb 9 oz. and cut to an even thickness of 2.5cm/1 inch

100 ml/scant ½ cup olive oil

2 garlic cloves, thinly sliced

3 sprigs of fresh rosemary

sea salt and freshly ground black pepper

extra virgin olive oil, for drizzling

TO SERVE

sautéed potatoes

rocket/arugula salad

lemon wedges (optional)

Serves 2

The traditional cut to use for this classic Tuscan recipe, known locally as Bistecca alla Fiorentina, is a T-bone steak, marinated overnight in olive oil and garlic and cooked over a hot grill or barbecue. It's a real treat for any meat lover!

Trim the excess fat off the edge of the steak, leaving a little if liked, and pat the steak dry with paper towels. Pour the olive oil into a shallow dish and add the garlic and rosemary. Turn the steak in the oil, ensuring there is some garlic and rosemary on each side.

steak Niçoise

Fillet steak provides a tasty alternative to tuna in this Provençal-inspired salad, which makes the perfect summer lunch.

½ teaspoon coarse sea salt

1 teaspoon black peppercorns

1 teaspoon dried rosemary

400 g/14 oz. fillet steak

2 tablespoons olive oil

200 g/1¼ cups fine green beans, trimmed

12 anchovy fillets

milk, for soaking (optional)

100 g/1½ cups rocket/arugula or mixed salad leaves

250 g/2¼ cups cherry or mini plum tomatoes, halved

75 g/scant ½ cup black olives marinated in oil and herbs

a handful of chopped fresh basil leaves or flat-leaf parsley, to serve

DRESSING

1 teaspoon Dijon mustard

2 tablespoons white wine vinegar

110 ml/scant 1 cup olive oil

sea salt and freshly ground black pepper

Serves 4

Put the salt, peppercorns and rosemary in a mortar and pound with a pestle until finely ground. Trim the excess fat off the beef and pat dry with paper towels, then roll it in the ground salt, pepper and rosemary until evenly coated.

Heat the oil in a large frying pan set over medium–high heat. Add the steak and cook on all sides for 5–6 minutes, turning every minute, depending on whether you want it rare or medium-rare. Set aside to cool, then cover and chill in the refrigerator for at least 1 hour.

Meanwhile, bring a saucepan of water to the boil and cook the green beans for 10 minutes. Rinse in cold water and drain.

Taste the anchovies, and if they are excessively salty, soak them in just enough milk to cover for 15 minutes. Drain and pat dry, then cut in half lengthways.

To make the dressing, put the mustard, vinegar and some salt and pepper in a bowl and whisk together. Gradually whisk in the olive oil until the dressing has a thick consistency.

Once the beef is well chilled, slice it thinly with a sharp knife. Assemble the salad on individual plates, starting with a layer of rocket/arugula, a few beans and some tomatoes. Next lay on the beef slices and anchovies. Give the dressing another whisk and spoon over the salad. Dot the olives and basil leaves around the salad and serve immediately.

whole chicken roasted on the barbecue

Cooking with the lid on your barbecue creates the same effect as cooking in a conventional oven. If you don't have a barbecue with a lid, you can cut the chicken in half and cook on the grill for about 15 minutes on each side.

1.5 kg/3 lb 5 oz. whole chicken
1 lemon, halved
4 garlic cloves, peeled
a small bunch of fresh thyme
extra virgin olive oil
sea salt and freshly ground black pepper

Serves 4–6

Wash the chicken thoroughly under cold running water and pat dry with paper towels.

Rub the chicken all over with the halved lemon, then put the lemon halves inside the body cavity with the garlic and thyme. Rub a little olive oil into the skin and season with salt and pepper.

Preheat the barbecue and when the coals are ready, rake them into two piles and carefully place a drip tray in the middle. Remove the grill rack and brush or spray it with oil. Return it to the barbecue and put the chicken on the rack above the drip tray. Cover with a lid, then cook over medium hot coals for 1 hour or until the skin is golden, the flesh is cooked through and the juices run clear when the thickest part of the meat is pierced with a skewer. If any bloody juices appear, cook for a little longer.

Let the chicken rest for 10 minutes before serving.

olive-infused chicken *with charred lemons*

This delicious concoction of olives, lemons, fresh marjoram and succulent chicken makes an ideal main course for a barbecue party. Serve with a selection of salads, such as tomato and basil.

1.5 kg/3 lb 5 oz. chicken
75 g/⅓ cup pitted black olives
4 tablespoons extra virgin olive oil
1 teaspoon sea salt
2 tablespoons chopped fresh marjoram
freshly squeezed juice of 1 lemon
plus 2 halved lemons
freshly ground black pepper

Serves 4

To prepare the chicken, put it onto a board with the back facing upwards and, using kitchen scissors, cut along each side of the backbone and remove it completely. Using your fingers, gently ease the skin away from the flesh, then put the chicken into a large, shallow dish. Put the olives, olive oil, salt,

marjoram and lemon juice into a separate bowl and mix well, then pour over the chicken and push as many of the olives as possible up between the skin and flesh of the chicken. Let marinate in the refrigerator for 2 hours.

Preheat the barbecue, then cook cut-side down over medium-hot coals for 15 minutes. Using tongs, turn the chicken over and cook for a further 10 minutes or until the skin is

golden, the flesh is cooked through and the juices run clear when the thickest part of the meat is pierced with a skewer. If any bloody juices appear, cook for a little longer. While the chicken is cooking, add the halved lemons to the grill and cook for about 10–15 minutes until charred and tender on all sides.

Let the chicken rest for 10 minutes before serving with the charred lemons.

To make the tapenade, put the olives, anchovies, garlic, capers, mustard and oil in a food processor and blend to form a fairly smooth paste. Season to taste with pepper. Transfer to a dish, cover and chill until needed.

Put the chicken, garlic, rosemary, lemon zest and juice, egg yolk, breadcrumbs and some salt and pepper in a food processor and blend until smooth. Transfer the mixture to a bowl, cover and marinate in the refrigerator for 30 minutes. Divide the mixture into 4 portions and shape into patties.

Cut the aubergine/eggplant into 12 slices and the courgettes/zucchini into 12 thin strips. Brush with olive oil and season with salt and pepper. Barbecue the vegetables for 2–3 minutes on each side until charred and softened. Keep them warm.

Meanwhile, brush the chicken patties lightly with olive oil and barbecue for 5 minutes on each side until charred and cooked through.

Toast the focaccia and top each slice with radicchio or rocket/arugula leaves, patties and grilled vegetables. Spoon over some tapenade and serve hot.

open chicken burger
with grilled vegetables

This open-faced sandwich is full of the flavours of Mediterranean cooking, with chargrilled vegetables, focaccia bread and salty olive tapenade.

750 g/1 lb 10 oz. skinless, boneless chicken breasts, minced/ground

2 garlic cloves, crushed

1 tablespoon chopped fresh rosemary

freshly grated zest and juice of 1 lemon

1 egg yolk

50 g/½ cup dried breadcrumbs or matzo meal

1 medium aubergine/eggplant

2 courgettes/zucchini

4 slices focaccia

radicchio or rocket/arugula leaves

olive oil, for brushing

sea salt and freshly ground black pepper

TAPENADE

125 g/⅔ cup black olives, pitted

2 anchovies in oil, drained

1 garlic clove, crushed

2 tablespoons capers, rinsed

1 teaspoon Dijon mustard

4 tablespoons extra virgin olive oil

freshly ground black pepper

Serves 4

sage-rubbed pork chops

Although pork should not be served rare, it is quite easy to overcook it, leaving the meat dry and tough. A good test is to pierce the meat with a skewer, leave it there for a second, remove it and carefully feel how hot it is – it should feel warm, not too hot or too cold, for the perfect result.

2 tablespoons chopped fresh sage
2 tablespoons wholegrain mustard
2 tablespoons extra virgin olive oil
4 large pork chops
sea salt and freshly ground black pepper
ready-made fresh tomato salsa, to serve

Serves 4

Put the sage, mustard and olive oil into a bowl and mix well. Season with a little salt and pepper, then spread the mixture all over the chops. Let marinate in the refrigerator for 1 hour.

Preheat the barbecue to hot, then cook the chops over hot coals for 2½–3 minutes on each side until browned and cooked through. Serve hot with fresh tomato salsa.

turmeric lamb fillet
with couscous salad

There are two cuts of lamb fillet that can be used for this dish; one is from the eye of the cutlets and is truly melt-in-the-mouth, but expensive. The other is from the neck: it's more marbled with fat and far cheaper. For best results, it is worth investing in the best cut of lamb you can find to really make the most of this recipe.

TURMERIC LAMB

3 teaspoons ground turmeric

1 teaspoon ground cinnamon

3 teaspoons medium curry powder

2 garlic cloves, chopped

3 tablespoons olive oil

4 tablespoons clear honey

1.5 kg/3 lb 5 oz. lamb fillets, neck or eye

sea salt and freshly ground black pepper

COUSCOUS SALAD

375 g/1½ cups couscous

½ teaspoon saffron threads

25 g/2 tablespoons butter

2 tablespoons olive oil

4 onions, sliced

1 garlic clove, chopped

100 g/⅔ cup shelled pistachio nuts, coarsely chopped

grated zest and freshly squeezed juice of 2 lemons

a bunch of fresh coriander/cilantro, chopped

sea salt and freshly ground black pepper

Serves 8

Put the turmeric, cinnamon, curry powder, garlic, oil and honey into a bowl, add salt and pepper to taste and stir well. Trim any excess fat off the lamb fillets and rub the spice mixture all over them. Transfer to a dish, cover and let marinate in the refrigerator overnight.

Meanwhile, put the couscous and saffron in a large bowl. Pour over 400 ml/1⅔ cups boiling water, mix and set aside for 15 minutes until all the liquid has been absorbed.

Meanwhile, heat the butter and oil in a large frying pan set over medium heat, add the onions and cook for 8 minutes until golden. Add the garlic and cook for 2 minutes, then add the onions and garlic to the prepared couscous. Add the pistachios, lemon zest and juice, coriander/cilantro and salt and pepper to taste, mix well and set aside.

Preheat the barbecue and cook the lamb fillets over hot coals for about 25 minutes, turning frequently and basting with any extra marinade. Cut the meat into slices and divide between serving plates. Serve hot with a generous helping of the couscous salad.

lamb and porcini skewers *with sage and Parmesan*

Rural feasts in Italy often involve grilling and roasting outdoors. One of the most exciting times is the mushroom season, when entire villages hunt for wild mushrooms and gather together to cook them. These kebabs/kabobs are prepared with freshly picked porcini, but you could substitute them with dried porcini reconstituted in water or field mushrooms.

450 g/1 lb. tender lamb, from the leg or shoulder, cut into bite-sized chunks
2 tablespoons olive oil
freshly squeezed juice of 1–2 lemons
leaves from a bunch of fresh sage, finely chopped (reserve a few whole leaves)
2 garlic cloves, crushed
4–8 fresh medium-sized porcini mushrooms, cut into quarters or thickly sliced
sea salt and freshly ground black pepper

TO SERVE:
truffle oil, for drizzling
shavings of Parmesan cheese
toasted sourdough bread
sun-blushed tomatoes

Serves 4

Put the lamb pieces in a bowl and toss in the oil and lemon juice. Add the sage and garlic and season with salt and pepper. Cover and leave to marinate in the refrigerator for about 2 hours.

Thread the lamb onto skewers adding a quarter, or slice, of porcini every so often with a sage leaf. Brush with any of the marinade left in the bowl. Preheat the barbecue to hot. Cook the kebabs/kabobs over hot coals for 3–4 minutes on each side.

Drizzle with truffle oil and scatter with Parmesan shavings. Serve immediately with toasted sourdough and sun blushed tomatoes.

souvlaki *with bulgur wheat salad*

Souvlaki is the classic Greek kebab/kabob, a delicious combination of cubed lamb marinated in red wine with herbs and lemon juice. The meat is tenderized by the wine, resulting in a juicy and succulent dish.

Trim the excess fat off the lamb and then cut the meat into 2.5-cm/1-inch cubes. Put into a shallow, non-metal dish. Add the rosemary, oregano, onion, garlic, wine, lemon juice, olive oil, and some salt and pepper. Toss well, cover and let marinate in the refrigerator for 4 hours. Return to room temperature for 1 hour before cooking.

To make the salad, soak the bulgur wheat in warm water for 30 minutes until the water has been absorbed and the grains have softened. Strain well to extract any excess water and transfer to a bowl. Add the remaining ingredients, season to taste and set aside for 30 minutes to develop the flavours.

Thread the lamb onto large rosemary stalks or metal skewers. Preheat the barbecue to hot and cook over hot coals for 10 minutes, turning and basting from time to time. Let rest for 5 minutes, then serve with the salad.

1 kg/2 lb 4 oz. lamb neck fillets
1 tablespoon chopped fresh rosemary
1 tablespoon dried oregano
1 onion, chopped
4 garlic cloves, chopped
300 ml/1¼ cups red wine
freshly squeezed juice of 1 lemon
75 ml/⅓ cup olive oil
sea salt and freshly ground black pepper

BULGUR WHEAT SALAD
350 g/1½ cups bulgur wheat
25 g/scant ⅓ cup chopped fresh flat-leaf parsley
15 g/scant ½ cup fresh mint leaves, chopped
2 garlic cloves, crushed
150 ml/⅔ cup extra virgin olive oil
freshly squeezed juice of 2 lemons
a pinch of caster/granulated sugar

Serves 6

butterflied lamb *with white bean salad*

This is the most delicious way to cook lamb on the barbecue.

To make the marinade, put the herbs, bay leaves garlic and lemon zest in mortar and grind to a paste with a pestle. Put the mixture in a bowl with the peppercorns and olive oil. Put the lamb into a shallow dish, pour over the marinade, cover and let marinate in the refrigerator overnight. Return to room temperature before cooking.

To make the salad, put the onion in a colander, sprinkle with salt and drain over a bowl for 30 minutes. Refresh under cold water and dry well. Transfer to a bowl, then add the beans, garlic, tomatoes, olive oil, vinegar, parsley and salt and pepper to taste.

Preheat the barbecue to medium-hot and cook for 12–15 minutes on each side until charred outside but pink in the middle. Let the lamb rest for 10 minutes then cut into slices and serve hot on top of the salad with a generous helping of salsa verde.

1.5–2 kg leg of lamb, butterflied

HERB, LEMON AND GARLIC MARINADE
leaves from 2 sprigs of fresh rosemary
leaves from 2 sprigs of fresh thyme
4 bay leaves
2 garlic cloves, coarsely chopped
pared zest of 1 lemon
1 teaspoon cracked black peppercorns
1 cup extra virgin olive oil

WHITE BEAN SALAD
1 large red onion, finely chopped
3 x 400-g/14-oz cans haricot beans, drained and rinsed
2 garlic cloves, chopped
3 tomatoes, deseeded and chopped
75 ml/scant ⅓ cup extra virgin olive oil
1½ tablespoons red wine vinegar
2 tablespoons chopped fresh flat-leaf parsley
sea salt and freshly ground black pepper
ready-made salsa verde, to serve

Serves 8

Spanish-style skewers

Meat and fish (the old-fashioned surf 'n' turf) can work well together and this recipe is a perfect example of this balance of strong flavours. It's best to use the chorizo sausage that needs cooking, rather than the cured tapas variety, although either would do.

300 g/10½ oz. uncooked chorizo

24 large, uncooked, peeled prawns/shrimp, deveined

24 large sage leaves

2 tablespoons extra virgin olive oil

freshly squeezed juice of 1 lemon

freshly ground black pepper

Serves 6

Cut the chorizo into 24 slices about 1 cm/½ inch thick and thread onto skewers, alternating with the prawns/shrimp and sage leaves. Put the olive oil and lemon juice into a small bowl, mix well, then drizzle over the skewers. Sprinkle with pepper.

Meanwhile, preheat a stove-top grill pan/griddle or barbecue to hot. Cook the skewers for 1½–2 minutes on each side until the chorizo and prawns/shrimp are cooked through. Serve immediately.

barbecued fish *bathed in oregano and lemon*

Greece is known for its simple and delicious cuisine made from fresh ingredients with seafood often being the highlight of any menu. This is a typical Greek dish of char-grilled bream with oil, oregano and garlic, but you could use other small fish such as red mullet, snapper or even trout.

grated zest of 1 and freshly squeezed juice of 2 lemons

250 ml/1 cup extra virgin olive oil

1 tablespoon dried oregano

2 garlic cloves, finely chopped

2 tablespoons chopped fresh flat-leaf parsley

6 snapper or bream, about 350 g/12 oz. each, well cleaned and scaled

sea salt and freshly ground black pepper

Serves 6

Put the zest and juice of 1 lemon in a small bowl. Add the olive oil, reserving 4 tablespoons, the oregano, garlic, parsley, and some salt and pepper. Leave to infuse for at least 1 hour.

Wash and dry the fish inside and out. Using a sharp knife, cut several slashes into each side. Squeeze the juice from the remaining lemon into a bowl, add the remaining 4 tablespoons of oil, some salt and pepper and rub the mixture all over the fish.

Heat a stove-top grill pan/griddle or barbecue, add the fish and cook for 3–4 minutes on each side until charred and cooked through. Put the fish on a large, warmed serving platter, pour over the dressing and let rest for 5 minutes before serving.

grilled sardines
with salmoriglio sauce

The smell of silvery blue sardines on a grill is unmistakable – it is one of the most appetizing scents in outdoor cooking. Sardines grill very well because they are an oily fish and are self-basting. Great shoals of them are to be found in Mediterranean waters in May and June, which is the best time to eat them. They are eaten grilled or fried, boned or stuffed, always with gusto!

12 large fresh sardines
olive oil

SALMORIGLIO SAUCE
2 tablespoons red wine vinegar
1–2 teaspoons granulated sugar
grated zest and freshly squeezed juice of ½ lemon
4 tablespoons good olive oil
1 garlic clove, finely chopped
1 tablespoon crumbled dried oregano
1 tablespoon salted capers, rinsed and chopped
lemon wedges, to serve

Serves 4

To make the salmoriglio, put the vinegar and sugar in a bowl and stir to dissolve. Add the lemon zest and juice. Whisk in the olive oil, then add the garlic, oregano and capers. Set aside to infuse.

Using the back of a knife, scale the sardines, starting from the tail and working towards the head. Slit open the belly and remove the insides, then rinse the fish and pat dry. Clip off any fins you don't want to see. Brush the fish with olive oil and arrange on a grill rack (there are racks especially made in a wheel shape for sardines).

Preheat a grill/broiler or barbecue to hot and cook for about 3 minutes on each side until sizzling hot and charring. Serve with the salmoriglio spooned over the top, with lots of lemon wedges for squeezing.

swordfish *with salsa*

Swordfish is brought to life with this delicious half-cooked salsa. Slow-roasting softens the tomatoes and intensifies their flavour. It's also great served on a bowl of fresh pasta such as ravioli.

500 g/1 lb 2 oz. cherry tomatoes
2 red onions, finely chopped
½ teaspoon crushed dried chillies/chiles
a large bunch of chopped fresh flat-leaf parsley
6 tablespoons olive oil

freshly squeezed juice of 2 limes
8 swordfish steaks, 100 g/3½ oz. each
sea salt and freshly ground pepper

Serves 8

Preheated oven at 150°C (300°F) Gas 2.

To make the salsa, put the tomatoes into a roasting pan and cook in the oven for 1 hour. Remove and let cool. Transfer them to a bowl, add the onions, dried chillies/chiles, parsley, oil, lime juice salt and pepper.

Season the swordfish steaks with salt and pepper. Preheat the barbecue to medium-hot and cook the fish for 4–6 minutes on each side, or until just cooked through. Serve with the salsa.

barbecued prawns/shrimp *with lemon*

For extra flavour and aroma, always grill prawns/shrimp with their shells on. Toss them in olive oil before adding to the barbecue and cook just until the flesh is just opaque – don't overcook or they will be dry and tasteless.

2 kg/4 lb 8 oz. tiger prawns/shrimp, shells on
about 6 tablespoons olive oil
4 lemons or 6 limes, cut into wedges, to serve

Serves 8

Put the prawns/shrimp into a large bowl or plastic bag, pour over the olive oil and shake to coat. Cook on a preheated barbecue until the shells are red and the flesh is opaque, then serve immediately with lemon or lime wedges for squeezing.

mixed griddled fish
with romesco sauce

Preheat the oven to 180°C (350°F) Gas 4.

To make the sauce, soak the peppers in warm water. Put the tomatoes in a roasting pan, drizzle with 1 tablespoon of the olive oil and sprinkle with the sugar and salt and pepper to taste. Roast in the preheated oven for about 20 minutes, or until soft.

Tear the bread into smallish chunks and toss with 2 tablespoons of the olive oil, the garlic and the almonds. Spread out evenly in a roasting pan and roast in the preheated oven for about 10 minutes, or until the bread and almonds are golden brown.

Put the roasted tomatoes in a food processor. Drain the soaked peppers and add them to the tomatoes, then blend until everything is chopped. Add the bread and almond mixture and blend to a coarse paste. Stir in the sherry vinegar, the dried chilli/hot pepper flakes and the remaining olive oil. Season with salt and pepper to taste and set aside.

Score a crisscross pattern on the squid tubes with a very sharp knife. Brush the squid, salmon and cod with 1 tablespoon of the olive oil each. Heat a stove-top grill pan/griddle to hot, then cook the seafood for 2–3 minutes on each side, adding the squid tentacles after a couple of minutes. The fish should be just cooked in the centre and the squid should be golden and tender. Put the remaining olive oil, the garlic, lemon juice and parsley in a bowl, season with salt and mix well. Spoon this over the griddled fish and serve immediately with the romesco sauce.

Sherry vinegar is the essential ingredient that lifts this fabulous Spanish sauce. It is the perfect accompaniment to tasty grilled mixed seafood in this classic Mediterranean recipe.

400 g/14 oz. baby squid, cleaned
4 small pieces of salmon fillet
4 small pieces of cod
4 tablespoons extra virgin olive oil
1 garlic clove, peeled and crushed
freshly squeezed juice of 1 lemon
a small bunch of fresh flat-leaf parsley, chopped
sea salt and freshly ground black pepper

ROMESCO SAUCE
2 dried sweet peppers
6 plum tomatoes, halved
60 ml/¼ cup extra virgin olive oil
a pinch of caster sugar
2 large slices of good country-style bread, crusts removed
2 garlic cloves, peeled and crushed
50 g/⅓ cup whole blanched almonds
2–3 tablespoons sherry vinegar
a pinch of dried chilli/hot pepper flakes, or to taste

Serves 4

stuffed char-grilled sardines

This dish is best made with good-sized plump, fresh sardines, which are slit from head to tail with the backbone removed. Full of delicious Mediterranean flavours, this is a great recipe for outdoor cooking on the barbecue while enjoying the summer sunshine.

4 large fresh sardines
2 tablespoons olive oil
4–6 spring onions/scallions, finely sliced
2–3 garlic cloves, crushed
1 teaspoon cumin seeds, crushed
1 teaspoon ground sumac
1 tablespoon pine nuts
1 tablespoon raisins, soaked in warm water for 15 minutes and drained
a small bunch of fresh flat-leaf parsley finely chopped
sea salt and freshly ground black pepper

FOR BASTING
3 tablespoons olive oil
freshly squeezed juice of 1 lemon
1–2 teaspoons ground sumac

Serves 4

To prepare the sardines, gently massage the area around the backbone to loosen it. Using your fingers, carefully prise out the bone, snapping it off at each end, while keeping the fish intact. Rinse the fish and pat it dry before stuffing.

Heat the oil in a heavy-based frying pan and stir in the spring onions/scallions until soft. Add the garlic, cumin and sumac. Stir in the pine nuts and pre-soaked raisins, and fry until the pine nuts begin to turn golden. Toss in the parsley and season with salt and pepper. Leave to cool.

Place each sardine on a flat surface and spread the filling inside each one. Seal the fish by threading them onto skewers.

Mix together the olive oil, lemon juice and sumac and brush some of it over the sardines. Preheat the barbecue to hot. Cook the stuffed fish for 2–3 minutes on each side, basting them with the rest of the olive oil mixture. Serve immediately.

Sicilian-spiced seabass *with grilled tomatoes and baby fennel*

An impressive dish that is easy to cook on the barbecue. If whole fish don't appeal, you could make this recipe with tuna or swordfish steaks.

1 generous teaspoon fennel seeds
1 generous teaspoon dried oregano
1 teaspoon cumin seeds
1 teaspoon sea salt
1 teaspoon green or black peppercorns
¼ teaspoon dried chilli/hot pepper flakes
6 small seabass, cleaned
extra virgin olive oil
3 lemons
a small handful of bay leaves
4 baby fennel bulbs
350 g/12 oz. cherry tomatoes
wedges of lemon, to serve

Serves 6

Crush the fennel seeds, oregano, cumin seeds, salt, peppercorns and dried chilli/hot pepper flakes together thoroughly in a mortar with a pestle. Make 3 slashes in each side of the fish with a sharp knife. Brush the fish with olive oil and rub the pounded spices over the fish and into the slits. Cut 2 of the lemons in half vertically, then cut 1½ into thin slices. Cut or tear the bay leaves into halves or thirds. Place a slice of lemon and a piece of bay leaf in each slit.

Cut each fennel bulb in quarters lengthways and thread the cherry tomatoes onto skewers. Brush the fish, fennel and tomatoes with oil. Preheat the barbecue and cook over medium heat until charred on both sides and cooked through. Serve immediately with lemon wedges for squeezing.

barbecued courgettes/zucchini

These are perfect to serve with meat or fish dishes.

8 courgettes/zucchini, cut lengthways into 1-cm/¼-inch slices
olive oil
balsamic vinegar
sea salt and freshly ground black pepper

Serves 8

Preheat the barbecue and cook the courgette/zucchini slices over medium heat for 3–4 minutes on each side, until lightly charred. Remove to a serving plate and sprinkle with olive oil, vinegar, salt and pepper. Serve hot, warm or cold.

barbecued salmon steaks *with basil and Parmesan butter*

Flavoured butters help to keep the fish deliciously moist, but be sure to watch the steaks carefully while cooking, as they can easily overcook.

To make the basil and Parmesan butter, beat the butter until soft. Gradually mix in the Parmesan, vinegar, basil and pepper to taste. Scoop onto a piece of wet parchment paper and roll into a cylinder. Wrap in plastic wrap and refrigerate (or freeze) for at least 1 hour, or until firm.

Put the marinade ingredients in a wide, shallow dish, mix well, then add the salmon steaks

and turn to coat well. Cover and let marinate for 20–30 minutes. Lift the steaks from the marinade and pat dry with paper towels.

Preheat the barbecue to medium–hot. Lightly oil the grill bars, add the salmon and barbecue for about 3 minutes on each side until crisp and brown on the outside and just opaque all the way through. Top with slices of the chilled, flavoured butter and serve immediately.

6 fresh salmon steaks, cut about 2.5 cm/1 inch thick

BASIL AND PARMESAN BUTTER
175 g/1 stick plus 3 tablespoons unsalted butter
25 g/¼ cup finely grated Parmesan cheese
1 teaspoon balsamic or sherry vinegar
25 g/½ cup chopped fresh basil leaves
freshly ground black pepper

MARINADE
1 large garlic clove, crushed
150 ml/¾ cup light olive oil
2 tablespoons balsamic or sherry vinegar
1–2 sprigs of fresh thyme, crushed

Serves 6

grilled polenta

Grilled polenta triangles make a lovely accompaniment for grilled meats and fish or they can be used as a base for grilled vegetables.

2 teaspoons sea salt
175 g/1¼ cup instant polenta
2 garlic cloves, crushed
1 tablespoon chopped fresh basil
50 g/3½ tablespoons butter
50 g/½ cup finely grated Parmesan cheese
freshly ground black pepper
olive oil, for brushing

a rectangular cake pan,
23 x 30 cm/9 x 12 inches, greased

Serves 8

Pour 1 litre water into a heavy-based saucepan and bring to the boil. Add the salt and gradually whisk in the polenta in a steady stream, using a large, metal whisk.

Cook over low heat, stirring constantly with a wooden spoon for 5 minutes or until the grains have swelled and thickened. Remove the saucepan from the heat and immediately beat in the garlic, basil, butter and Parmesan until the mixture is smooth. Pour into the greased cake pan and let cool completely.

Preheat the barbecue to hot. Turn out the polenta onto a board and cut into large squares, then cut in half again to form triangles. Brush the triangles with a little olive oil and cook over hot coals for 2–3 minutes on each side until charred and heated through.

barbecued artichokes

Try to find small or baby artichokes for this dish so that they can be cooked straight on the barbecue without any blanching first.

18 small artichokes
1 lemon, halved
2 tablespoons extra virgin olive oil
sea salt and freshly ground black pepper
lime wedges, to serve

CHILLI LIME MAYONNAISE
1 dried chipotle chilli/chile
2 egg yolks
300 ml/1¼ cups olive oil
freshly squeezed juice of 1 lime
sea salt

Serves 6

To make the mayonnaise, cover the dried chilli/chile with boiling water and let soak for 30 minutes. Drain and pat dry, then cut in half and scrape out the seeds.

Finely chop the chilli/chile flesh and put in a food processor. Add the egg yolks and a little salt and blend briefly until frothy. With the blade running, drizzle the oil through the funnel until the sauce is thick and glossy. Add the lime juice and, if the mayonnaise is too thick, a tablespoon of warm water. Taste and adjust the seasoning, then cover and set aside.

Trim the stalks from the artichokes and cut off the top 2 cm/¾ inch of the globes. Slice the globes in half lengthways, cutting out the central 'choke' if necessary. Rub the cut surfaces all over with lemon juice to stop them discolouring.

Toss the artichokes with the oil and a little salt and pepper. Preheat the barbecue to medium-hot and cook for 15–20 minutes, until charred and tender, turning halfway through the cooking time. Serve with the mayonnaise and wedges of lime.

summer vegetable skewers
with home-made pesto

Full of sunshine flavours, these kebabs/kabobs can be served with pasta tossed in some of the pesto sauce. Home-made pesto is very personal – some people like it very garlicky, others prefer lots of basil or Parmesan – so simply adjust the quantities to suit your taste.

2 aubergines/eggplant, cut into chunks
2 courgettes/zucchini, cut into chunks
2–3 bell peppers, cut into chunks
12–16 cherry tomatoes
4 red onions, quartered

FOR THE MARINADE
4 tablespoons olive oil
freshly squeezed juice of ½ a lemon
2 garlic cloves, crushed
1 teaspoon sea salt

FOR THE PESTO
3–4 garlic cloves, roughly chopped
leaves from a large bunch of fresh basil (at least 30–40 leaves)
½ teaspoon sea salt
2–3 tablespoons pine nuts
extra virgin olive oil, as required
60 g/⅔ cup finely grated Parmesan cheese

Serves 4–6

To make the pesto, use a mortar and pestle to pound the garlic with the basil leaves and salt. Add the pine nuts and pound them to a paste. Slowly drizzle in some olive oil and bind with the grated Parmesan. Continue to pound and grind with the pestle, adding in enough oil to make a smooth sauce. Set aside.

Put all the prepared vegetables in a bowl. Mix together the olive oil, lemon juice, garlic and salt and pour it over the vegetables. Using your hands, toss the vegetables gently in the marinade, then thread them onto skewers.

Preheat the barbecue to medium-hot. Cook the kebabs/kabobs for 2–3 minutes on each side, until the vegetables are nicely browned. Serve the kebabs/kabobs with the pesto on the side for drizzling.

food to go

bruschetta *with baby mozzarella and cherry tomatoes*

Bruschetta toppings are easy to make and very versatile. Many work well stirred into pasta or rice, or blended to make a dip. This recipe is an update on the classic mozzarella, tomato and basil salad, which originally came from the island of Capri, off the coast of Italy. It makes a delicious appetizer or light lunch. Try using authentic Italian buffalo mozzarella to make this recipe extra special.

200 g/7 oz. baby mozzarella cheeses, drained and halved

250 g/1¼ cups halved cherry tomatoes

4 tablespoons extra virgin olive oil, plus extra to serve

1 ciabatta loaf, left out overnight to dry out, if possible

1 large garlic clove, unpeeled and halved

50 g/⅔ cup rocket/arugula

sea salt and freshly ground black pepper

balsamic vinegar, to serve

Serves 4

Put the mozzarella and tomatoes in a large bowl, add the olive oil, season with salt and pepper and mix well. Cover and leave to marinate for 1–2 hours.

When ready to serve, slice the bread open lengthways. Preheat a stove-top grill pan/griddle and cook both sides over medium–high heat until toasted. Alternatively, toast the bread under a preheated medium grill/broiler. Rub the toasted bread with the garlic and drizzle with olive oil. Toss the rocket/arugula with the mozzarella and tomato and spoon onto the toasted bread. Drizzle with balsamic vinegar and serve immediately.

mixed mushroom frittata

With its lovely, earthy flavours, a frittata is an Italian version of the Spanish tortilla or the French omelette and different ingredients are added depending on the region or season.

3 tablespoons extra virgin olive oil
2 shallots, finely chopped
2 garlic cloves, finely chopped
1 tablespoon chopped fresh thyme leaves
300 g/10½ oz. mixed wild and cultivated mushrooms, such as girolle, chanterelle, portobello, shiitake and cep, washed
6 eggs
2 tablespoons chopped fresh flat-leaf parsley
sea salt and freshly ground black pepper

Serves 6

Heat 2 tablespoons of the oil in a large non-stick frying pan set over low heat. Add the shallots, garlic and thyme and cook for 5 minutes until softened. Chop or coarsely slice the mushrooms and add to the pan. Fry for 4–5 minutes until just starting to release their juices. Remove from the heat.

Put the eggs into a bowl with the parsley and a little salt and pepper, whisk briefly, then stir in the mushroom mixture. Wipe the frying pan clean with paper towels.

Heat the remaining oil in the clean pan and pour in the egg and mushroom mixture. Cook over medium heat for 8–10 minutes until set on the bottom. Transfer to a preheated grill/broiler and cook for about 2–3 minutes until the top is set. Leave to cool and serve at room temperature.

4 large pita breads

water and olive oil, to moisten the bread

2 teaspoons chopped fresh oregano, or 1 teaspoon dried oregano, crushed

2 tablespoons freshly squeezed lemon juice

½ onion, coarsely grated

2 tablespoons extra virgin olive oil

500 g/1 lb 2 oz. lean pork or lamb (usually leg meat), cut into 2.5 cm/1 inch cubes

salad, such as lettuce or cabbage, finely sliced

1 cucumber, sliced

1 red bell pepper, sliced

12 cherry tomatoes

12 radishes, halved

1 red onion, sliced into rings

GARLIC DRESSING

100 ml/scant ½ cup thick, strained plain yogurt

4 garlic cloves, chopped and crushed

a 5-cm/2-inch piece of cucumber, coarsely grated, then squeezed dry

½ teaspoon sea salt

Serves 4

souvlaki in pita

Souvlaki is the Greek equivalent of the kebab/kabob, a street food traditionally eaten at festival time. These days, it is mostly made of pork (though lamb is used when in season). Loved by locals and travellers alike, it is inexpensive, filling and delicious, with its yogurt, garlic and cucumber dressing and hot, soft pita bread. In Greece, the local bread is often briefly pan-fried; at home it is better to brush pita bread with oil and water and bake briefly, or put it under the grill/broiler to warm. Although pita bread comes from the Middle East, not Greece, it 'pockets' beautifully, making the perfect receptacle for a meat and salad snack.

Preheat the oven to 180°C (350°F) Gas 4.

Preheat a stove-top grill pan/griddle or barbecue. Put the oregano, lemon juice, grated onion and olive oil in a bowl and mash with a fork. Add the cubed meat and toss well. Cover and let marinate for 10–20 minutes. Drain, then thread the meat onto metal skewers. Cook on the preheated stove-top grill pan/griddle or barbecue for 5–8 minutes, or until golden and cooked through.

While the meat is cooking, brush or sprinkle the pita breads all over with the water and oil and bake in the preheated oven for 3–5 minutes or long enough to soften the bread, but not dry it. Cut off a strip from the long side, then pull open and part the sides of the breads to make a pocket. Push the strip inside. Keep the breads warm.

Put the salad ingredients in a bowl, toss gently, then insert into the pockets of the pita breads.

To make the dressing, put the yogurt in a bowl, then beat in the garlic, cucumber and salt. Add a large spoonful to each pocket.

Remove the hot, cooked meat from the skewers, then push it into the pockets. Serve immediately, while the meat and bread are hot and the salad cool.

pizzette *with assorted meaty and veggie toppings*

You can serve these mini pizzas with any variety of toppings. Sautéed onions, dolcelatte and rocket/arugula is another great combination.

PIZZA DOUGH

250 g/2 cups plain/all-purpose flour

½ x 7-g package or 1½ level teaspoons fast-action dried yeast

½ teaspoon sea salt

5 tablespoons olive oil

175 ml/⅔ cup hand-hot water

TOPPINGS

1 small aubergine/eggplant, thinly sliced

1 onion, thinly sliced

pinch of fresh thyme leaves

4 generous teaspoons sun-dried tomato paste

75 g/½ cup cherry tomatoes, quartered

125 g/4 oz. dolcelatte or gorgonzola cheese, crumbled

8 slices of pepperoni

handful of black olives

100 g/3½ oz. mozzarella cheese, diced

2 teaspoons ready-made pesto

2 canned artichoke hearts, sliced

2 tablespoons semi-dried tomatoes

fresh basil leaves

a handful of rocket/arugula

sea salt and freshly ground black pepper

Makes 4 mini pizzas

To make the pizza dough, mix together the flour, yeast and salt in a large bowl. Add 2 tablespoons of the olive oil and the water and mix to a soft dough. Lightly dust the work surface with flour, tip the dough out of the bowl and knead for 5 minutes, or until smooth and elastic. Shape the dough into a neat, smooth ball, return to the bowl and cover with plastic wrap. Leave in a warm place for 1 hour, or until doubled in size.

Heat 2 tablespoons of the oil in a frying pan and fry the aubergine/eggplant on both sides until golden, then remove from the heat. In another pan, heat the remaining oil and gently fry the onion until very tender and just starting to turn golden. Add the thyme and remove from the heat.

Preheat the oven to 230°C (450°F) Gas 8.

Divide the dough into 4 evenly sized pieces and shape each piece into a pizza about 15 cm/6 inches in diameter. Place on a solid baking sheet, then spread sun-dried tomato paste over 2 of the pizzas. Top one pizza with the aubergine/eggplant slices, cherry tomatoes and half the crumbled dolcelatte. Top the other pizza with pepperoni, olives and half the diced mozzarella.

For the third pizza, spread the pesto over the base and arrange the artichoke hearts and semi-dried tomatoes on top. Scatter over the remaining mozzarella. Garnish with basil leaves. Top the last pizza with the sautéed onions and remaining dolcelatte. Season all the pizzas well with salt and pepper and cook on the top shelf of the preheated oven for about 5 minutes, or until golden. Top the onion pizza with the rocket/arugula and serve immediately.

assorted focaccia crostini

Focaccia is one of the tastiest breads to make, and so easy that it's a crime not to bake it yourself. Make this focaccia in advance then slice just before serving and add the assorted toppings.

500 g/4 cups (strong) white bread flour, plus extra for kneading

7-g/¼-oz. package or 3 level teaspoons fast-action dried yeast

1 teaspoon fine sea salt

4 tablespoons extra virgin olive oil, plus extra for drizzling

300 ml/1¼ cups hand-hot water

2 tablespoons fresh rosemary leaves

2 generous teaspoons coarse sea salt

GARLIC MUSHROOMS

1 tablespoon olive oil

1 tablespoon unsalted butter

1 shallot, finely chopped

250 g/8 oz. mixed wild mushrooms

1 tablespoon chopped flat-leaf parsley

1 garlic clove

MEDITERRANEAN TOMATOES

4 ripe tomatoes

1 roasted red bell pepper, from a jar

1 tablespoon fresh basil leaves, torn

1 tablespoon mixed olives, pitted and chopped

100 g/3½ oz. buffalo mozzarella cheese, torn

1 garlic clove

BEANS & MINT

175 g/1⅓ cups broad/fava beans and/or peas

1 tablespoon chopped fresh mint

grated zest of ½ lemon

100 g/3½ oz. feta cheese, crumbled

1 garlic clove

baking pan, 20 x 30 cm/8 x 12 inches

Serves 4–6

Mix together the flour, yeast and fine salt in a large bowl. Add 1 tablespoon of the olive oil and the water and mix to a soft dough. Lightly dust the work surface with flour, tip the dough out of the bowl and knead for 10 minutes, or until smooth and elastic. Shape the dough into a neat, smooth ball, return to the bowl and cover with plastic wrap. Leave in a warm place for 1 hour, or until doubled in size. Lightly oil the baking pan. Dust the work surface with flour, tip the dough out and knead for 30 seconds. Roll the dough into a rectangle to fit in the baking pan. Lay the dough inside the pan. Cover with oiled plastic wrap and leave in a warm place for about 1 hour, or until doubled in size. Preheat the oven to 220°C (425°F) Gas 7. Dimple the surface of the dough with your fingertips, drizzle the remaining olive oil all over it and scatter the rosemary and coarse salt over the top. Bake in the preheated oven for about 20 minutes, or until golden brown and well risen. Let cool in the pan for about 10 minutes, then transfer to a wire rack. Cut the focaccia into finger-width slices, toast both sides on a stove-top grill pan/griddle and top with one of the following toppings.

For garlic mushrooms, heat the oil and butter in a frying pan, add the shallot and cook over medium heat until translucent. Add the mushrooms, season, cook until tender and stir through the parsley. Rub the garlic clove over the toasted bread and pile the mixture on top. Drizzle with olive oil. Serve warm.

For Mediterranean tomatoes, chop the tomatoes and red pepper. Add the basil and olives and gently stir through the mozzarella. Rub the garlic clove over the toasted bread and pile the mixture on top. Drizzle with olive oil. Serve hot.

For beans & mint, cook the beans in lightly salted boiling water until tender. Drain and refresh under cold water. Drain well, then put in a food processor and blend to a coarse purée. Stir in the mint, lemon zest and feta, and season. Rub the garlic clove over the toasted bread and pile the mixture on top. Drizzle with olive oil. Serve hot.

focaccia *topped with cherry tomatoes and pesto*

15 g/¼ oz. fresh yeast or ½ tablespoon
easy-blend dried yeast

a pinch of sugar

350 g/2⅔ cups plain/all-purpose flour,
plus extra for kneading

1 tablespoon sea salt, plus extra
for cooking

2 tablespoons extra virgin olive oil,
plus extra for drizzling

175 g/scant 1 cup halved cherry tomatoes

40 g/⅓ cup black olives, pitted and halved

PESTO

25 g/½ cup basil leaves

1 garlic clove, crushed

2 tablespoons pine nuts

6 tablespoons extra virgin olive oil

2 tablespoons finely grated
Parmesan cheese

sea salt and freshly ground
black pepper

a baking pan, 20 x 30 cm/8 x 12 inches

Serves 8

The secret to making focaccia is to let the dough rise three times rather than twice, as for regular bread dough. It is well worth the extra 30 minutes needed, as the result is light, airy and totally moreish!

Preheat the oven to 200°C (400°F) Gas 6.

Put the yeast into a small bowl, add the sugar and 225 ml/scant 1 cup warm water and stir until the yeast has dissolved. Add 2 tablespoons of the flour and leave in a warm place for 10 minutes until frothy.

Sift the remaining flour and the 1 tablespoon salt into the bowl of an electric mixer fitted with a dough hook and add the frothed yeast mixture and oil. Mix for 10 minutes until smooth and elastic. Shape into a ball, transfer to an oiled bowl, cover with plastic wrap and let rise for 1 hour or until doubled in size.

Transfer the dough to a lightly floured surface, knead gently, then shape or roll into a rectangle to fit snugly into the baking pan. Cover and let rise for 30 minutes.

Using your fingers, press indentations all over the surface of the dough. Cover again and let rise for a further 1 hour until well risen.

Meanwhile, to make the pesto, put the basil leaves, garlic, pine nuts and olive oil into a food processor and purée to form a vivid green paste. Transfer to a bowl and stir in the cheese and salt and pepper to taste.

Spread 2–3 tablespoons of the pesto carefully over the risen dough without letting it collapse. Add the tomatoes and olives and sprinkle with a little more oil and about ½ tablespoon sea salt. Bake for 25 minutes until risen and golden. Leave to cool on a wire rack and serve warm.

Note Store the remaining pesto in an airtight container in the refrigerator for up to 3 days and use as a pasta sauce.

chicken salad wrap

These speedy chicken salad wraps are perfect for lunch on the go or for a picnic with friends on a warm summer's day.

4 soft flour tortillas
4 tablespoons mayonnaise
2 teaspoons wholegrain mustard
2 cooked chicken breasts, shredded
2 carrots, grated
a wedge of white cabbage, finely sliced
2 medium tomatoes, finely sliced
sea salt and freshly ground black pepper

Serves 4

Lay each tortilla flat on a piece of parchment paper. Spread with the mayonnaise and mustard. Add the shredded chicken, grated carrot, sliced cabbage and tomato and season with salt and pepper.

Roll up the tortillas into tight cylinders, using the parchment paper to help you. Twist the ends of the paper together.

Cut the cylinders in half diagonally. Wrap each portion in plastic wrap and chill until needed

Note These wraps are great for using up leftovers. Any extra chicken, meat, fish, boiled eggs, potatoes, pasta, rice or roasted vegetables such as pumpkin, peppers or onions can be incorporated to make a wonderfully simple but delicious lunch.

pan bagnat

Traditionally pan bagnat, from Nice in the South of France, is made in a large baguette, but this recipe is delicious made with Italian ciabatta rolls.

4 ciabatta rolls

2 garlic cloves, crushed

4 tablespoons extra virgin olive oil

1 tablespoon red wine vinegar

4 ripe tomatoes, thickly sliced

200 g/⅔ cup canned tuna in oil, drained and flaked

24 black olives, pitted

12 anchovy fillets in oil, drained

2 tablespoons capers in brine, rinsed

a few rocket/arugula leaves

a handful of basil leaves

sea salt and freshly ground black pepper

Serves 4

Cut the ciabatta rolls in half. Put the garlic, oil and vinegar in a bowl, mix well, then brush all over the cut surfaces of the rolls.

Divide the remaining ingredients between the 4 rolls, add the lids and wrap in plastic wrap. Leave to infuse for at least 1 hour before serving.

arancini *with pecorino, porcini and mozzarella*

You can use leftover risotto for these rice balls if you happen to have any, but as they are so delicious it's worth making the risotto especially. They can be prepared and rolled in advance; coat them in breadcrumbs and fry just before serving.

15 g/½ oz. dried porcini mushrooms
1 tablespoon olive oil
2 tablespoons unsalted butter
2 shallots, finely chopped
1 large garlic clove, crushed
250 g/1¼ cups risotto rice
(arborio or carnaroli)
750–850 ml/3–3½ cups hot vegetable stock
40 g/⅓ cup finely grated pecorino cheese
1 tablespoon chopped fresh
flat-leaf parsley or oregano
125 g/4 oz. mozzarella cheese, diced
100 g/¾ cup plain/all-purpose flour
2 eggs, lightly beaten
200 g/2 cups fresh, fine breadcrumbs
about 1 litre/4 cups sunflower oil, for frying
sea salt and freshly ground black pepper

Makes 15–18

Soak the porcini in a small bowl of boiling water for about 15 minutes, or until soft. Drain well on paper towels and finely chop.

Heat the olive oil and butter in a medium saucepan and add the shallots, garlic and chopped porcini. Cook over low–medium heat until soft but not coloured. Add the rice to the pan and stir to coat well in the buttery mixture. Gradually add the vegetable stock, one ladleful at a time, adding more as the stock

is absorbed by the rice, stirring as you do so. Continue cooking in this way until the rice is al dente and the stock is used up. Remove the pan from the heat, add the pecorino and herbs and season with salt and pepper. Tip the risotto into a bowl and let cool completely.

Once the rice is cold, divide it into walnut-sized pieces and roll into balls. Taking one ball at a time, flatten it into a disc in the palm of your hand, press some diced mozzarella in the middle and wrap the rice around it to completely encase the cheese. Shape into a neat ball. Repeat with the remaining risotto.

Tip the flour, beaten eggs and breadcrumbs into separate shallow bowls. Roll the rice balls first in the flour, then coat well in the eggs and, finally, roll them in the breadcrumbs to completely coat.

Fill a deep-fat fryer with sunflower oil or pour oil to a depth of about 5 cm/2 inches into a deep saucepan. Heat until a cube of bread

sizzles and browns in about 5 seconds. Cook the arancini, in batches, in the hot oil for 3–4 minutes or until crisp, hot and golden brown. Drain on paper towels and serve immediately.

cheesy stuffed croissants

A great portable snack, best made with your favourite cheese such as Gruyère or brie. This is the classic recipe, but you can also use sliced tomatoes or mushrooms.

4 croissants
2 teaspoons Dijon mustard
4 slices cheese (of your choice)
4 thick slices Black Forest smoked ham
freshly ground black pepper

Serves 4

Preheat the oven to 180°C (350°F) Gas 4.

Cut the croissants in half lengthways and open out. Spread each croissant with ½ teaspoon Dijon mustard, then add the cheese, ham and pepper.

Transfer to a baking sheet and cook in the preheated oven for 10 minutes. Serve hot or cold.

stuffed picnic loaf

Great for a picnic – a loaf packed with barbecued vegetables, pesto and goat cheese. Make it a day ahead to give the flavours time to develop.

1 round loaf of bread, about 23 cm/9 inches diameter, 10 cm/4 inches high
2 tablespoons extra virgin olive oil
ready-made pesto
2 large red onions, cut into wedges
2 large red bell peppers
2 large courgettes/zucchini, sliced
250 g/9 oz. soft goat cheese, diced
12 large basil leaves
sea salt and freshly ground black pepper

Serves 6

Cut the top off the loaf and carefully scoop out most of the bread, leaving just the outer shell. Put 1 tablespoon of the oil into a bowl, stir in the pesto and spread half the mixture around the inside of the shell and lid. Set aside.

Brush the onions with a little of the remaining oil and cook on a preheated stove-top grill pan/griddle or barbecue for 10 minutes on each side until very tender. Let cool.

Char-grill the peppers on the grill pan/griddle or barbecue for about 15 minutes until blackened all over. Transfer to a plastic bag and let cool. Peel away the skin, discard the seeds and cut the flesh into quarters, reserving any juices.

Brush the sliced courgettes/zucchini with oil and cook as above for 2–3 minutes on each side until charred and softened. Let cool.

Layer the filling inside the loaf, with the goat cheese and remaining pesto in the middle and the basil on top. Sprinkle with any remaining oil and the pepper juices and replace the lid. Wrap the loaf in plastic wrap and put on a plate. Top with a board and a weight or heavy food can and chill in the refrigerator overnight. The next day, cut into wedges and serve.

spicy meat pastries

These are intricate little pastries with sweet and sour flavours and delicious aromas. Traditionally fried, they can also be baked.

175 g/1 cup plus 4 tablespoons plain/all-purpose flour
½ teaspoon sea salt
2 tablespoons olive oil
90 ml/scant ⅓ cup water
1 egg yolk, lightly beaten

FILLING
3–4 tablespoons olive oil
1 large onion, finely chopped
200 g/7 oz. lean minced/ground lamb
1 teaspoon ground allspice
1 teaspoon ground cumin
a large pinch of ground cinnamon
freshly squeezed juice of 1 lemon
3 tablespoons raisins, rinsed

150 ml/scant ⅔ cup hot water
3 tablespoons finely chopped fresh mint leaves
2 tablespoons pine nuts, toasted
sea salt and freshly ground black pepper

a round 8 cm/3½ inch pastry cutter

Makes about 30

Preheat the oven to 200°C (400°F) Gas 6.

To make the pastry, sift the flour and salt into a bowl. Make a well in the centre, add the oil and mix with your fingers. Add the water and knead until a soft, neat ball is formed. Cover with plastic wrap and let rest for 30 minutes.

Heat the oil in a saucepan, add the onion and cook for about 10 minutes until it turns light brown. Increase the heat and add the lamb, turning and breaking up the lumps until all the moisture has evaporated and it starts to sizzle. Add the allspice, cumin, cinnamon, salt and pepper and brown for 2–3 minutes. Add the lemon juice, raisins and the hot water, cover and cook for 20 minutes. It should be a fairly dry mixture by then. Add the mint and pine nuts and set aside.

Divide the pastry in half. Put one piece on a lightly floured surface and roll out thinly to a circle about 30 cm/12 inches diameter, turning the pastry frequently. Cut out rounds with the pastry cutter. Gather the remaining pastry from around the discs and add it to the remaining portion of pastry. Knead until soft again, cover and set aside.

Fill a small bowl with cold water. Put 1 teaspoon of filling in the middle of a round of pastry. Dip a finger in the water and wet the edges, then fold half of the pastry over the other half, making a half-moon shape. Press the edges firmly to seal and put it on a greased baking sheet. Repeat until all the rounds have been used. Roll out the remaining pastry, cut out more rounds and repeat the process.

Brush the tops with the egg yolk and bake in the preheated oven for 10–12 minutes until golden. Serve warm or at room temperature.

onion, thyme and goat cheese tarts

What is it about caramelized onions? They smell just divine, especially when cooked in butter. These simple onion tarts, topped with creamy goat cheese, are best served warm, although they are also good cold.

40 g/3 tablespoons butter
500 g/1 lb 2 oz. onions, finely sliced
2 garlic cloves, crushed
1 tablespoon chopped fresh thyme leaves
350 g/12 oz. ready-made puff pastry, defrosted if frozen
flour, for rolling out
a 200-g/7-oz. log goat cheese

Makes 8

Preheat the oven to 220°C (425°F) Gas 7.

Melt the butter in a frying pan set over low heat. Add the onions, garlic and thyme and fry gently for 20–25 minutes, until softened and golden. Let cool.

Put the pastry onto a lightly floured surface and roll out to form a rectangle, 20 x 40 cm/ 8 x 16 inches. Cut the rectangle in half lengthways and into 4 crossways, making 8 pieces, each about 10 cm/4 inches square.

Divide the onion mixture between the squares, leaving a thin border around the edges. Cut the cheese into 8 slices and arrange in the centre of each square.

Put the pastries on a baking sheet and bake in the preheated oven for 12–15 minutes until the pastry has risen and the cheese is golden. Serve warm.

simple tomato and olive tart *with Parmesan*

Basil oil is particularly good sprinkled onto this simple pastry, but you can use ordinary olive oil. Preheating the baking sheet will make the base of the tart beautifully crisp.

To make the basil oil, blanch the leaves very briefly in boiling water, drain and dry thoroughly with paper towels. Put into a blender, add the oil and salt and blend until very smooth. Strain the oil through a very fine sieve/strainer. Keep in the refrigerator but return to room temperature before using.

Preheat the oven to 220°C (425°F) Gas 7 and put a baking sheet on the middle shelf.

Roll out the dough on a lightly floured surface to form a rectangle, 25 x 30 cm/10 x 12 inches. Trim the edges and transfer the dough to a second baking sheet. Using the blade of a sharp knife, gently tap the edges several times (this will help the pastry rise and the edges separate) and prick all over with a fork.

Put the tomatoes, olives, basil oil, salt and pepper into a bowl and mix lightly. Spoon the mixture over the pastry and carefully slide the tart directly onto the preheated baking sheet. Bake for 12–15 minutes until risen and golden.

Remove from the oven and sprinkle with the Parmesan. Cut into quarters and serve hot with rocket/arugula leaves.

350 g/12 oz. ready-made puff pastry, thawed if frozen
125 g/⅔ cup halved red cherry tomatoes
125 g/⅔ cup halved yellow cherry tomatoes
50 g/⅓ cup semi-dried or sun-dried tomatoes, halved
50 g/⅓ cup black olives, pitted and halved
2 tablespoons basil oil (below)
25 g/⅓ cup shaved Parmesan cheese
sea salt and freshly ground black pepper
a handful of rocket/arugula leaves, to serve

BASIL OIL
25 g/½ cup fresh basil leaves
150 ml/⅔ extra virgin olive oil
a pinch of sea salt

Serves 4

traditional cheese pies

These delicious cheese pies are part of Greek tradition and hail from the island of Alonnisos. Every family has their own secret recipe that has been passed down through generations. These pies are so simple and delicious, they are sensational eaten straight out of the frying pan. In Greece they are often eaten for breakfast but they are also perfect for serving as part of a lunch accompanied by a fresh green or tomato salad.

250 g/2 cups plain/all-purpose flour
a pinch of sea salt
2 teaspoons olive oil,
plus 6–7 tablespoons for frying
150 ml/⅔ cup cold water
225 g/8 oz. feta cheese
2 tablespoons extra virgin olive oil

Serves 6–12

Sift the flour and salt into a bowl, add the 2 teaspoons olive oil and the water and mix until it becomes an elastic, neat ball. Transfer to a floured work surface and start stretching and kneading with the palm of your hand for 5 minutes. Cover with plastic wrap and let rest for at least 30 minutes.

Divide the dough in two and roll out the pieces, one at a time, on a floured surface into a large circle, preferably using a thin rolling pin. Keep turning the dough round and over, sprinkling with a little flour, until you have a thin circle of about 60 cm/24 inches diameter.

Crumble half the cheese all over the circle, sprinkle with 1 tablespoon olive oil and start folding the pie. First roll the two diametrically opposite sides like two fat cigars until they meet at the centre. Holding one end of the pastry down, roll the opposite end around it.

Heat the oil in a large frying pan set over medium heat, lift the cheese pie with a flat spatula and slide it into the pan. Fry until light golden on the underside, then turn it over carefully and fry it on the other side. The whole frying operation is swift and it takes about 6–7 minutes. Remove and put on a plate lined with paper towels. Repeat with the remaining pastry and serve immediately.

Preheat the oven to 190°C (375°F) Gas 5.

To make the filling, put the spinach in a large saucepan of water, cover and cook gently for 5–6 minutes, stirring occasionally, until wilted. Drain the spinach in a colander and set aside. Wipe the saucepan dry, add the olive oil and cook the onion and spring onions/scallions until translucent. Add the spinach, salt and pepper and cook for 4–5 minutes. Let cool a little. Beat the eggs in a large bowl, crumble in the cheese, add the herbs, milk and spinach mixture and mix well.

Unroll the pastry carefully – you will have a rectangular stack of paper-thin sheets. Brush the roasting pan with the hot melted butter. Butter sparingly the top sheet of pastry and lay it into the pan, folding any excess on one side (keep in mind that the pastry will shrink when cooked). Continue the same way, folding the excess on alternate ends until you have used about half the pastry. Add the filling and spread it evenly. Fold the sides over it and start covering with the remaining pastry sheets, brushing each with the melted butter.

Finally, brush the top layer of pastry generously with butter. Using a sharp knife, score the top layers of pastry into diamond or square shapes – do it carefully to avoid spilling the filling. Using your fingertips, sprinkle a little cold water on top to stop the pastry curling.

Bake in the preheated oven for 50 minutes until golden on top. Slice carefully and serve hot or at room temperature.

spinach and cheese pie

Pastries are at the heart of Greek food and culture and each village and every island has its own indigenous versions that act like a showcase to local produce. This sensational pie is the most common and most delicious. It may seem time-consuming, but it will make a lot of people happy.

500 g/6 cups fresh spinach
4 tablespoons extra virgin olive oil
1 large onion, finely chopped
4–5 spring onions/scallions, trimmed and coarsely chopped
4 eggs
250 g/9 oz. feta cheese
90 g/2 cups chopped fresh dill
3–4 tablespoons chopped fresh flat-leaf parsley
4 tablespoons milk
400-g/14-oz. package filo pastry, thawed if frozen
150 g/1 stick plus 2 tablespoons butter, melted
sea salt and freshly ground black pepper

a roasting pan, 35 x 30 cm/14 x 12 inches

Serves 12

Roquefort and walnut tart

Blue cheese imparts a wonderful richness of flavour to this light creamy tart with walnut pastry. It makes a perfect appetizer served with a salad made from rocket/arugula, pears and walnuts.

15 g/scant ⅓ cup walnuts
100 g/¾ cup plain/all-purpose flour
1 teaspoon sea salt
50 g/3½ tablespoons butter, diced

ROQUEFORT FILLING
100 g/3½ oz. Roquefort cheese
200 g/¾ cup ricotta cheese
150 ml/⅔ cup double/heavy cream
3 eggs, lightly beaten
2 tablespoons walnut oil
sea salt and freshly ground black pepper

ROCKET/ARUGULA SALAD
50 g/½ cup walnuts
2 ripe pears
200 g/scant 3 cups rocket/arugula
a handful of fresh flat-leaf parsley
4 tablespoons walnut oil
2 tablespoons olive oil
2 teaspoons sherry vinegar
1 teaspoon clear honey
sea salt and freshly ground black pepper

parchment paper and baking beans or rice
23-cm/9-inch flan pan, buttered

Serves 6

To make the pastry, put the walnuts in a dry frying pan and cook for 1–2 minutes until toasted. Transfer to a bowl and let cool. When cool, transfer to a food processor or blender and process until fine. Sift the flour and salt into a bowl and rub in the butter until the mixture resembles fine breadcrumbs. Stir in the ground walnuts and then enough cold

water to form a soft dough, about 1–2 tablespoons. Transfer the dough to a lightly floured surface, knead gently, then shape into a flat disc. Wrap in plastic wrap and chill for about 30 minutes.

Preheat the oven to 200°C (400°F) Gas 6. Transfer the dough to a lightly floured surface, roll out to a disc about 25 cm/10 inches in diameter and line the flan pan with the pastry. Prick the base with a fork and chill for a further 30 minutes. Remove from the refrigerator and line the pastry case with parchment paper and baking beans or rice. Bake in the preheated oven for 10 minutes. Remove the paper and beans or rice and bake for a further 5–6 minutes until the pastry is crisp and lightly golden. Remove from the oven and let cool.

Meanwhile, to prepare the filling, dice the Roquefort and put in a food processor. Add the ricotta, cream, eggs, walnut oil, salt and pepper and blend briefly until mixed but not smooth. Pour into the pastry case and cook for about 20 minutes until risen and golden. Let cool slightly in the pan.

To make the salad, put the walnuts in a dry frying pan and toast until golden. Remove, cool and chop coarsely. Peel, core and slice the pears and put into a bowl. Add the rocket/arugula, parsley and walnuts.

Put the walnut oil into a measuring cup, add the olive oil, sherry vinegar, honey, salt and pepper and whisk well. Pour over the salad, toss gently, then serve with the warm tart.

tomato, cucumber, onion and feta salad

Summers in Greece would not be complete without this salad, which can be a meal in itself. In Greek, it is called Horiatiki salata, which means 'peasant or country salad'.

Cut the tomatoes in quarters lengthways and cut out the stalk pieces. Cut the quarters into bite-sized wedges and put in a bowl.

Add the onion, green pepper, cucumber, feta cheese, olives, olive oil, oregano, salt and pepper and toss to coat. Keep at room temperature for at least 30 minutes before serving to let the flavours develop.

400 g/14 oz. ripe tomatoes
1 small red onion, thinly sliced
1 green bell pepper, sliced
a 10-cm/4-inch piece of cucumber, thinly sliced
150 g/5½ oz. feta cheese, crumbled
6–8 black or green olives
5–6 tablespoons extra virgin olive oil
a large pinch of dried oregano
sea salt and freshly ground black pepper

Serves 6

bean salad
with mint and Parmesan

This salad can be served as as part of a tapas spread or light lunch. It also works well as an appetizer or snack, too. If it's early in the season and you have young, tender broad beans, it's not necessary to peel them after blanching. Out of season, you can use frozen broad beans or flat beans cut into 2.5-cm/1-inch lengths.

750 g/1 lb 10 oz. podded, young fresh or frozen broad/fava beans
3 heads of chicory
leaves from 3 sprigs of fresh mint
25 g/⅓ cup shaved Parmesan cheese
sea salt

HAZELNUT OIL DRESSING
2 tablespoons extra virgin olive oil
4 tablespoons hazelnut oil
2 teaspoons white wine vinegar
1 teaspoon Dijon mustard
¼ teaspoon sugar
sea salt and freshly ground black pepper

Serves 6

Plunge the broad beans into a saucepan of lightly salted, boiling water, return to the boil and simmer for 1–2 minutes. Drain and refresh the beans immediately under cold running water. Pat dry and peel away the grey-green outer skin if necessary. Put the peeled beans into a salad bowl.

Cut the chicory in half lengthways, slice thickly crossways, then add to the beans. Add the mint leaves, tearing any large ones in half. Using a potato peeler, cut thin shavings of Parmesan over the salad.

Just before serving, put the dressing ingredients into a small jug, mix well, sprinkle over the salad, toss well, then serve immediately.

salad box

Very simple and flexible, this lunch box can include any leftovers you have in your refrigerator.

1 aubergine/eggplant, sliced lengthways

4 courgettes/zucchini, sliced lengthways

400-g/14-oz. can butter/lima beans, rinsed and drained

300 g/1½ cups cooked penne pasta

4 tomatoes, sliced

4 hard-boiled/hard-cooked eggs, halved

a bunch of fresh flat-leaf parsley, chopped

4 tablespoons caperberries, or 4 teaspoons capers, rinsed and drained

4 tablespoons olive oil

2 tablespoons balsamic vinegar

100 g/1¼ cups shaved Parmesan cheese

1 lemon, quartered

sea salt and freshly ground black pepper

Serves 4

Cook the aubergines/eggplant and courgettes/zucchini on a stove-top grill pan/griddle over medium heat for 5 minutes on each side.

Divide the butter beans and cooked pasta between 4 lunch boxes. Add the aubergines/eggplant, courgettes/zucchini, tomatoes, boiled eggs, parsley and caperberries or capers.

Sprinkle the salads with the olive oil and balsamic vinegar. Season with salt and pepper and top with shavings of Parmesan. Add a wedge of lemon to each box, put on the lids and chill overnight. Serve at room temperature.

pasta, squash and feta salad *with olive dressing*

You can use the recipe on page 42 to make your own tapenade. For a speedy alternative, ready-made tapenade is available from most deli counters is usually quite good quality.

Peel and deseed the butternut squash and cut the flesh into bite-sized pieces. Put into a bowl or plastic bag, then add the oil, thyme, salt and pepper, Toss well, then arrange in a single layer in a roasting pan. Roast in a preheated oven at 200°C (400°F) Gas 6 for about 25 minutes until golden and tender. Let cool.

To make the dressing, put the olive oil, tapenade, lemon juice and honey into a bowl. Whisk well, then add salt and pepper to taste.

Bring a large saucepan of lightly salted water to the boil, add the penne and cook according to the package instructions. Drain well, then immediately stir in 4 tablespoons of the dressing. Let cool.

When cool, put the pasta and squash into a salad bowl, mix gently, then add the feta cheese, cherry tomatoes, basil and toasted pumpkin seeds. Just before serving, stir in the remaining dressing and serve immediately.

750 g/1½ lb butternut squash
1 tablespoon extra virgin olive oil
1 tablespoon chopped fresh thyme leaves
500 g/1 lb dried penne
350 g/10 oz. feta cheese, diced
350 g/1⅔ cups halved cherry tomatoes
4 tablespoons chopped fresh basil
4 tablespoons pumpkin seeds, toasted
sea salt and freshly ground black pepper

DRESSING
150 ml/⅔ cup extra virgin olive oil
3 tablespoons tapenade (see page 42)
freshly squeezed juice of 1 lemon
1 teaspoon clear honey
sea salt and freshly ground black pepper

Serves 6

alfresco feasts

risotto *with* Sicilian pesto

Made with almonds, basil and tomato, this pesto recipe comes from Trapani in Sicily, where it is known as pesto trapanese. It is traditionally served with a regional pasta called busiate, which is similar to bucatini. The rich, smoky flavour of toasted almonds and the peppery flavour of the basil permeate the risotto rice, creating the perfect combination.

extra virgin olive oil, for frying, plus extra to serve
2 shallots, finely chopped
500 g/2⅓ cups risotto rice, preferably vialone nano
60 ml/¼ cup white wine
1 litre/4 cups hot vegetable stock

SICILIAN PESTO
75 g/⅔ cup toasted sliced almonds
80 g/1¾ cups fresh basil leaves
4 garlic cloves, lightly crushed
2 x 400-g/14-oz. cans whole plum tomatoes, drained, deseeded and chopped
125 ml/½ cup olive oil
75 g/¾ cup freshly grated pecorino cheese
sea salt and freshly ground black pepper

TO SERVE
toasted sliced almonds
freshly grated pecorino cheese

Serves 4

To make the pesto, put the almonds in a food processor with a pinch of salt and grind finely. Transfer to a large bowl.

Put the basil, garlic and tomatoes in a food processor and process to a paste. Add to the ground almonds and stir in the olive oil, pecorino cheese and a good grinding of salt and pepper to taste. Mix well and leave to rest for at least 2 hours.

Cover the base of a large, heavy-based pan with olive oil, heat gently and add the shallots and 2 tablespoons of water. Cook until the shallots are transparent. Add the rice, increase the heat and cook for 2 minutes, stirring continuously. Add the wine and let it evaporate, then reduce the heat.

Level the rice and carefully spoon 10 ladles of freshly boiled stock over it. Cover with a lid and cook on low heat for 15 minutes. Next, add the pesto and stir energetically for 1 minute. Turn off the heat, cover and let stand for 4–5 minutes.

Serve the risotto in a serving large dish or individual plates. Drizzle it with olive oil and sprinkle with almond slices, then serve immediately with the pecorino cheese.

Note To toast your own almonds, place sliced almonds on a heavy baking sheet and bake in a preheated oven at 100°C (200°F) Gas Low for 30 minutes, or until golden brown. Remove from the sheet and let cool.

fennel and black olive risotto

This delicate fennel and lemon risotto has the taste of the Mediterranean stirred in just before serving. The rich earthiness of shiny, oven-dried black olives is wonderful, but if you prefer something less pungent, use large, juicy green olives instead.

FENNEL AND BLACK OLIVE RELISH
6 tablespoons extra virgin olive oil
1 onion, finely chopped
1 garlic clove, crushed
1 fennel bulb, trimmed and chopped
5 sun-dried tomatoes in oil, drained and coarsely chopped
200 g/1¼ cups oven-dried Greek-style olives, pitted
1 bay leaf
12 fresh basil leaves, torn
2 tablespoons aniseed liqueur, such as sambuca
sea salt and freshly ground black pepper

FENNEL RISOTTO
about 1 litre/4 cups vegetable or chicken stock
125 g/1 stick plus 1 tablespoon unsalted butter
1 onion, finely chopped
3 fennel bulbs, trimmed and finely chopped (green tops included)
finely grated zest of 1 lemon
300 g/1⅓ cups risotto rice
150 ml/⅔ cup dry white wine
freshly grated Parmesan cheese, to serve

Serves 6

To make the relish, heat 2 tablespoons of the olive oil in a medium saucepan and gently cook the onion, garlic and fennel for a few minutes, until softened. Add the sun-dried tomatoes, olives and bay leaf and continue to cook for 2–3 minutes more. Season to taste with salt and pepper, remove the bay leaf, then stir in the basil. Transfer to a food processor and blend to a coarse texture. Stir in the aniseed liqueur and remaining olive oil. Cover and set aside.

To make the risotto, put the stock in a saucepan and keep at a gentle simmer. Melt half the butter in another large, heavy saucepan and add the onion. Cook gently for 5 minutes, until soft, golden and translucent, but not browned. Stir in the fennel and lemon zest and continue to cook for 10 minutes, until softened. Add the rice and stir until well coated with the butter and heated through. Pour in the wine and boil hard until it has reduced and almost disappeared.

Begin adding the stock, a large ladleful at a time, stirring gently until each addition has almost been absorbed. The risotto should be kept at a bare simmer throughout cooking, and don't let the rice dry out – add more stock if necessary. Continue until the rice is tender and creamy, but the grains still firm and the fennel absolutely tender. (This should take 15–20 minutes, depending on the type of rice used – check the package instructions.)

Taste and season well with salt and pepper and beat in the remaining butter. Cover and let rest for a couple of minutes so the risotto can relax, then serve immediately. Just before serving, you may like to add a little more hot stock to loosen the risotto, but don't let it wait around too long or the rice will turn mushy. Top with the fennel and black olive relish, before serving with grated Parmesan.

1 kg/2 lb 4 oz. fresh clams, well scrubbed
400 g/14 oz. dried linguine or spaghetti
65 ml/¼ cup extra virgin olive oil
3 garlic cloves, roughly chopped
2 large red chillies/chiles, deseeded
and chopped
65 ml/¼ cup dry white wine
a handful of fresh flat-leaf parsley leaves,
roughly chopped
sea salt and freshly ground black pepper
crusty bread, to serve

Serves 4

Tap each clam lightly on the work surface and discard any that don't close.

Bring a large saucepan of lightly salted water to the boil and cook the pasta for 8–10 minutes, until al dente. Drain and return to the pan.

Meanwhile, heat the oil in a large saucepan over medium heat. Add the garlic and chillies/chiles and cook until the garlic just starts to sizzle, flavouring the oil without burning. Increase the heat to high, add the wine and cook until it boils and has reduced by half.

Add the clams, cover the pan tightly and cook for 3–4 minutes, shaking the pan to encourage the clams to open. Discard any clams that don't open.

Add the pasta to the pan, toss to combine and season to taste with salt and pepper. Stir in the parsley and serve immediately with good crusty bread on the side for mopping up the juices.

linguine *with clams and garlic*

This dish is often on the menu in restaurants in Italy, especially in coastal towns where good seafood is plentiful and inexpensive. It's one of those restaurant dishes that's easy to cook at home. Since it contains so few ingredients, quality and freshness are key. Look out for small clams, which are sweeter, and use a good, fruity extra virgin olive oil.

Sicilian spaghetti *with tomato sauce*

There are many variations of this classic Sicilian dish, known locally as pasta alla Norma after one of the composer Vincenzo Bellini's operas. The richness is balanced by the sharp flavour of grated ricotta salata, a salted and aged ewes' milk ricotta. Good alternatives are aged pecorino or even feta cheese.

Cut the aubergines/eggplant into small dice and put in a colander. Sprinkle with salt and put the colander on a plate. Set aside to drain for 30 minutes.

Meanwhile, dip the tomatoes in boiling water for 10 seconds, then drop into cold water. Slip off the skins, cut in half and squeeze out and discard the seeds. Chop the flesh coarsely.

Heat the olive oil in a frying pan/skillet, add the garlic, cook for 2–3 minutes until golden, then add the tomatoes. Cook for about 15 minutes until the tomatoes start to disintegrate.

Bring a large saucepan of salted water to the boil, add the spaghetti and cook according to the package instructions, about 8 minutes.

Meanwhile, rinse the aubergines/eggplant, drain and pat dry. Heat 2.5 cm/1 inch vegetable oil in a frying pan, add the aubergines/eggplant and fry until golden brown. Remove and drain on paper towels, then stir into the sauce.

Drain the pasta, reserving 2 tablespoons of the cooking water in the pan, and return the pasta to the hot pan. Stir in the tomato sauce, basil and grated cheese and serve.

3 medium aubergines/eggplant (round violet ones if possible)

500 g/1 lb 2 oz. very ripe red tomatoes (add 2 tablespoons of tomato purée/paste if it does not look red enough)

3 tablespoons olive oil

3 garlic cloves, chopped

350 g/12 oz. spaghetti or spaghettini

3 tablespoons chopped fresh basil

3–4 tablespoons freshly grated ricotta salata, aged pecorino or Parmesan cheese, plus extra to serve

sea salt and freshly ground black pepper

vegetable oil, for frying

Serves 4

grilled bell peppers *with balsamic and herb dressing*

Served raw in salads or as crudités, or roasted, grilled/broiled, fried or stewed, bell peppers add colour, texture and flavour to summer dishes. The red ones are the sweetest, followed closely by the orange and yellow ones. The green ones taste slightly bitter, but they can be used too.

4 red, yellow or orange bell peppers, halved lengthways and deseeded

4 tablespoons extra virgin olive oil

2 tablespoons balsamic vinegar

1 teaspoon coriander seeds, crushed

sea salt and freshly ground black pepper

TO SERVE

a few sprigs of fresh coriander/cilantro or flat-leaf parsley, finely chopped

75 g/2¾ oz. feta cheese, crumbled (optional)

Serves 4

Put the bell pepper halves in a bowl, add the olive oil, vinegar, coriander seeds, salt and pepper and mix well. Cover until required.

Preheat the barbecue. Put the bell pepper halves on the grill, cut side up, reserving the excess dressing. Cook until the skin starts to blister and brown, and the flesh is tender. Alternatively, cook them skin side up under a preheated hot grill/broiler. Scrape away the charred skin and discard. Transfer the pepper halves to a serving plate and spoon the reserved dressing over them. Sprinkle with the chopped coriander/cilantro or parsley and serve with crumbled feta cheese, if using.

tomato upside-down tart *with basil*

With its vivid red tomatoes and fresh green basil, this tart looks spectacular and is perfect for summer entertaining. The flavours are delicious too – the tomatoes bursting with flavour, the garlic softly singing and layers of crisp pastry melting in every mouthful. It is very simple to prepare, and makes an ideal starter or light lunch. Choose the best tomatoes you can find, and make sure they are perfectly ripe: they should feel heavy for their size and smell fragrant.

8–10 large ripe plum tomatoes (size depending on what will fit the pan)
2 garlic cloves, finely chopped
1 tablespoon dried oregano
4 tablespoons extra virgin olive oil, plus extra to serve
250 g/9 oz. puff pastry, thawed if frozen
sea salt and freshly ground black pepper
a good handful of basil leaves, to serve

a shallow tart pan or sauté pan,
22 cm/8¾ inches diameter

Serves 4

Preheat the oven to 160°C (325°F) Gas 3. Cut the tomatoes in half around the middle. Arrange cut side up in the shallow tart pan, so they fit tightly together. Mix the garlic and oregano with the olive oil, salt and pepper. Spoon or brush the mixture over the cut tomatoes.

Bake in the oven for about 2 hours, checking from time to time. The tomatoes should be slightly shrunk and still a brilliant red colour. If they get too dark, they will be bitter. Let cool in the pan (if it is very burned, wash it out, brush it with oil and return the tomatoes). Increase the oven temperature to 200°C (400°F) Gas 6.

Roll out the pastry to a circle slightly bigger than the pan. Using the rolling pin to help you, lift up the pastry and unroll it over the pan, letting the edges drape over the sides. Lightly press the pastry down over the tomatoes, but do not trim the edges yet. Bake for 20 minutes until golden.

Let settle for 5 minutes, then trim off the overhanging edges and invert onto a plate. Sprinkle with olive oil and basil leaves and serve.

spicy sausage and bell pepper pizza

Look for good-quality, authentic, stonebaked, pizza bases/crusts. For vegetarians, replace the sausages with baby artichokes.

Preheat the oven to 220ºC (425ºF) Gas 7. Spread the passata over the pizza bases/crusts and top with the rest of the ingredients. Bake in the preheated oven for about 15 minutes, until the sausage has cooked through and the bases/crusts are golden.

While the pizzas are cooking, prepare the salad. Put the rocket/arugula in a large bowl. Put the oil and vinegar in another bowl and whisk with a fork. Pour over the leaves and toss well. Season to taste with salt and pepper.

Serve the salad on the side or arrange in small mounds in the centre of each pizza. Serve immediately.

125 ml/½ cup passata/Italian sieved tomatoes
2 x 22-cm/8¾-inch good-quality, thin ready-made pizza bases/crusts
2 spicy Italian sausages, thinly sliced
2 balls of fresh mozzarella cheese
2 tablespoons sliced pickled jalapeños
1 large roasted or char-grilled red bell pepper in oil, thinly sliced

ROCKET/ARUGULA SALAD
4 large handfuls of rocket/arugula
1 tablespoon olive oil
2 teaspoons red wine vinegar
sea salt and freshly ground black pepper

Serves 4

pizza alla margherita

This is a very patriotic pizza – the colours represent the Italian flag. The lemon juice in the dough makes it light and crisp. If '00' or semolina flour are not available, use plain/all-purpose flour.

Put the bakestone or baking sheets in the oven and preheat to 220ºC (425ºF) Gas 7.

To make the dough, put the flour in a bowl, crumble the fresh yeast into the flour, add the lemon juice, olive oil and a generous pinch of salt, then add enough warm water to form a very soft dough. Transfer to a floured surface and knead for 10 minutes, or until smooth and elastic. Put the dough in a clean, oiled bowl (or an oiled plastic bag), cover and let rise until doubled in size (about 1 hour).

Cut the dough in half and knead each half into a round. Pat or roll the rounds into 25-cm/10-inch circles, keeping the bases well floured. Transfer the pizzas onto baking sheets lined with non-stick parchment paper. Spread each one lightly with passata or tomato sauce, cover with sliced mozzarella and season with salt and pepper. Let rise in a warm place for 10 minutes, then open the oven door and slide paper and pizza onto the hot bakestone or baking sheets. If you are brave, try to shoot them into the oven so that they leave the paper behind – this takes practice. Alternatively, use a baker's peel.

Bake for 18–20 minutes, until the crust is golden and the cheese melted but still white.

Remove from the oven, sprinkle with basil leaves and olive oil, then eat immediately.

Note Farina di semola is very finely ground and needs no extra flour. You can grind ordinary semolina into fine flour by processing it in a blender for about 2 minutes.

250 g/2 cups fine '00' or Italian semolina flour (farina di semola)
7 g/¼ oz. fresh yeast
1 tablespoon lemon juice
1 tablespoon olive oil
a pinch of salt
about 300 ml/1¼ cups warm water
125 ml/½ cup passata/Italian sieved tomatoes or ready-made tomato sauce
250 g/9 oz. fresh mozzarella, thinly sliced
a good handful of fresh basil leaves
extra olive oil, for trickling
sea salt and freshly ground black pepper

a 'testa' or terracotta bakestone, or 2 large heavy baking sheets
baking sheets lined with non-stick parchment paper
a baker's peel (optional)

Serves 4

Unlike most dishes cooked with cheese, this is light and elegant, and perfect to serve as a first course. Alternatively, make a meal of it with a simple green salad, or make individual tarts for a picnic.

To make the pastry, put the flour, butter and salt in a food processor and, using the pulse button, process until the butter is broken down (about 5–10 pulses). Add 3 tablespoons cold water and pulse just until the mixture forms coarse crumbs; add 1 more tablespoon if necessary, but do not do more than 10 pulses.

Transfer the pastry to a sheet of parchment paper, form into a ball and flatten to a disc. Wrap and refrigerate for 30–60 minutes.

Roll out the pastry on a floured work surface to a disc slightly larger than the tart pan. Carefully transfer the pastry to the pan, patching any holes as you go and pressing gently into the sides. To trim the edges, roll a rolling pin over the top, using the edge of the pan as a cutting surface, and let the excess fall away. Tidy up the edges and refrigerate until firm, about 30–60 minutes. Preheat the oven to 200°C (400°F) Gas 6.

Prick the pastry all over, line with the parchment paper and fill with beans or baking weights. Bake in the oven for 15 minutes, then remove the paper and weights and bake until just golden, about 10–15 minutes more. Let the tart shell cool slightly before filling.

To make the filling, put the eggs, crème fraîche/sour cream and a large pinch of salt in a bowl and whisk well. Slice each goat cheese into 3 rounds and arrange in the tart shell. Pour in the egg mixture and sprinkle with the Gruyère. Snip the chives with kitchen scissors and sprinkle over the top.

Bake in the preheated oven for 20–30 minutes, or until browned.

goat cheese tart

200 g/1⅔ cups plain/all-purpose flour, plus extra for rolling

100 g/3½ oz. cold unsalted butter, cut into pieces

a pinch of salt

3–4 tablespoons cold water

GOAT CHEESE FILLING

3 eggs

200 ml/¾ cup crème fraîche/sour cream

3 Crottin de Chavignol goat cheeses, about 50–75 g/1¾–2¾ oz. each

50 g/½ cup finely grated Gruyère cheese

a small bunch of fresh chives

fine sea salt

parchment paper and baking beans or baking weights

a loose-based tart pan, 27 cm/10¾ inches diameter

Serves 4–6

Provence-style artichokes *with bacon*

Globe artichokes, ranging from tiny to immense, from vivid green buds to purple-stippled balls, are an essential feature of Provençal cooking. Locals swear by them as life-enhancing, and claim that they cure indigestion, hangovers and even flu. Do not be put off by the intricacies of preparation; it is well worth the five minutes of effort because the eating is glorious.

4 large, bell-shaped globe artichokes
½ lemon
250 g/9 oz. smoked bacon pieces (lardons)
freshly ground black pepper (optional)
freshly grated nutmeg (optional)
100 ml/⅓ cup dry white Provençal wine
4 bay leaves
a handful of fresh flat-leaf parsley, chopped

Serves 4

Tear off and discard the two tough, outer base layers of leaves from the artichokes. Trim or peel the stems. Slice about 5 cm/2 inches off the pointed tops of the leaves. Cut each globe in half lengthways.

Use a spoon or a melon baller to dig out the fluffy choke. Discard this and the tiny leaves around it. Rub the lemon over all the cut surfaces. Prepare all the artichokes in the same way.

Heat a large, heavy-based saucepan or flameproof casserole dish until very hot. Sizzle the bacon until the fat runs, about 3 minutes.

Add some pepper and nutmeg (if using), the wine and bay leaves. Put the artichokes in the pan, cut side down. Cover tightly and cook over a high heat for 5 minutes. Rearrange the artichokes so that the top layer is now at the bottom. Cover and cook over a medium-low heat for 20–25 minutes more. Test the top layer: the artichoke flesh must be easy to pierce with a fork. Continue cooking if necessary. Top up with extra wine if it looks sparse.

Serve the artichokes hot or warm, sprinkled with the sauce and some chopped parsley.

Note Quarter the artichokes, if necessary, to fit them in the pan.

Provencal tian with tomato sauce

'Tian' is the Provençal name for a square earthenware dish, but if you use a non-stick roasting pan it still tastes great. Ideally, it should be served tepid or at room temperature. The tian will improve with age and can easily be made one day in advance.

To make the tomato sauce, heat the oil in a saucepan, add the garlic and cook until just soft, 1–2 minutes. Add the tomatoes, sugar, and salt to taste. Cover and simmer gently for 10 minutes. Remove the garlic cloves, stir in the basil and parsley and set aside.

Bring a large saucepan of water to the boil and add a pinch of salt. Add the aubergine/eggplant slices and cook until just blanched and tender, 3–5 minutes. Drain well.

Put the breadcrumbs, herbs and a pinch of salt in a bowl, stir well and set aside.

Preheat the oven to 200°C (400°F) Gas 6. Pour 3–4 tablespoons of the oil in the roasting pan or dish, arrange the aubergine/eggplant rounds on top and drizzle with some of the remaining oil. Top with the onion rings and sprinkle with salt and pepper. Dot the sauce on top, spreading as evenly as possible. Arrange the tomato slices on top and sprinkle with the breadcrumbs, followed by the olives. Bake in the oven until well browned, about 45 minutes. Serve hot or warm.

4 medium aubergines/eggplant, sliced crossways into 2-cm/¾-inch pieces
5 tablespoons fresh breadcrumbs
½ teaspoon herbes de Provence
about 125 ml/½ cup extra virgin olive oil
2 large onions, sliced into thick rings
3 large tomatoes, sliced (not beefsteak)
40 g/¼ cup pitted black olives, sliced
sea salt and freshly ground black pepper

TOMATO SAUCE
1 tablespoon extra virgin olive oil
3 garlic cloves
1.5 kg/3 lb 5 oz. tomatoes, skinned, deseeded and chopped
a pinch of sugar
a small handful of fresh basil, chopped
a small handful of fresh flat-leaf parsley, chopped
sea salt and freshly ground black pepper

non-stick roasting pan or earthenware dish

Serves 4–6

stuffed Greek aubergines/eggplant

The Greek name for this dish, papoutsakias, means 'little shoes' and they do, in fact, look a bit like slippers. It is often flavoured with basil leaves, but here oregano is used, that favourite of all Greek herbs.

2 large aubergines/eggplant (about 600–700 g/1 lb 5 oz–1 lb 9 oz.), halved lengthways
6 tablespoons extra virgin olive oil
6 garlic cloves, crushed
1 red or white onion, sliced into rings
6 firm-fleshed ripe red tomatoes, blanched, skinned, then cut into segments
2 celery stalks (optional), chopped
1 teaspoon dried oregano
4 tablespoons thick tomato purée/paste
sprigs of fresh oregano, marjoram or thyme (optional)

4 thin slices cheese, such as Greek kasseri, Cheddar or pecorino, about 50 g/1¾ oz. (optional)
sea salt and freshly ground black pepper

a baking dish big enough to hold the aubergines/eggplant in a single layer

Serves 4

Preheat the oven to 180°C (350°F) Gas 4. Using a sharp serrated knife, cut out the central flesh of the aubergine/eggplant halves, leaving a 1-cm/½-inch shell. Cut the flesh into 1-cm/½-inch chunks. Heat 4 tablespoons of the oil in a large frying pan/skillet and add the garlic and aubergine/eggplant halves, cut sides down. Cook over moderate heat for 5 minutes. Remove and place them, cut side up, in a baking dish. Bake in the oven for 15 minutes. Leave the oil and garlic in the pan.

Meanwhile, prepare the filling. Add the aubergine/eggplant cubes to the oil in the pan. Sauté for 5 minutes, then add the onion, tomatoes, celery (if using) and dried oregano, and cook over high heat. Add the remaining oil and cook, stirring constantly, until the cubes are fairly soft and the tomatoes reduced. Scoop up the aubergine/eggplant pieces with some of the other vegetables and pile them inside the part-cooked shells, then bake for a further 40 minutes.

Meanwhile, add the tomato purée/paste to the pan, then add 175 ml/¾ cup boiling water. Stir over gentle heat for 15 minutes to form a rich, fragrant sauce, then turn off the heat. Taste and season well with salt and pepper.

Test the aubergines/eggplant: the outer shells should be dark, wrinkled and soft. If not, cook them for another 20 minutes. Serve them hot, warm or at room temperature, with the sauce poured over and around. Top with the herbs and cheese (if using).

300 g/10½ oz. small aubergines/eggplants
4 tablespoons olive oil

PESTO
a large bunch of fresh basil
75 g/2¾ oz. pan-toasted pine nuts
1 garlic clove, roughly chopped
75 g/2¾ oz. Parmesan cheese, grated
6–8 tablespoons olive oil
sea salt and freshly ground black pepper

a baking sheet, lightly oiled

Serves 4

Preheat the oven to 190°C (375°F) Gas 5. Cut the aubergines/eggplants in half lengthways and put on the baking sheet. Drizzle with a little of the oil and bake in the oven for 15–20 minutes, then turn them over and cook for a further 15 minutes.

To make the pesto, put the basil, pine nuts, garlic, Parmesan, the remaining olive oil and seasoning in a blender, and process until smooth. When the aubergines/eggplants are cooked, drizzle with pesto. Serve hot or cold.

Top tip Make twice the quantity of pesto and store the extra in the fridge – it always comes in handy as an easy salad dressing, or tossed through pasta for a quick, delicious supper. Keep the pesto covered with a thin layer of olive oil and it will stay fresh for several weeks.

baked aubergines/ eggplant *with pesto sauce*

If you can find them, use the little Asian aubergines/ eggplants - they look very pretty and have a more interesting texture than large ones. When buying herbs, try going to independent stores or markets where they are sold in big bunches, like flowers. These herbs often taste nicer and are much better value.

sweet glazed bell pepper salad

Italians have been eating roasted bell peppers for centuries, and they are truly wonderful. Don't worry that there are too many in this recipe. They will all disappear!

10 red bell peppers, cut into large chunks and deseeded
5 red onions, quartered lengthways
4 tablespoons olive oil
5 tablespoons balsamic vinegar
2 tablespoons clear honey
400 g/2½ cups pitted kalamata or other black olives, chopped
sea salt and freshly ground black pepper
a sprig of fresh flat-leaf parsley, to serve

Serves 20

Preheat the oven to 180°C (350°F) Gas 4. Put the bell peppers and onions into a large bowl, add the olive oil and mix to coat. Transfer to 2 large roasting pans and cook in a preheated oven for 1 hour, turning the vegetables after 40 minutes so they will cook evenly. Add the vinegar, honey, olives, salt and pepper, mix well and set aside to cool. Serve warm or cold, topped with a sprig of parsley.

mozzarella-baked tomatoes

If you can find it, use purple basil, which looks even more spectacular than green. This dish really couldn't be easier, and makes a nice change from roasted tomato halves.

20 ripe tomatoes
250 g/9 oz. mozzarella cheese, drained and cut into 20 pieces
100 ml/⅓ cup olive oil
a bunch of fresh basil, torn
sea salt and freshly ground black pepper

a large baking sheet, lightly oiled

Serves 20

Preheat the oven to 160°C (325°F) Gas 3. Cut a deep cross, to about half way down, in the top of each tomato and stuff a piece of mozzarella into each. Transfer to the baking sheet and sprinkle with salt and pepper. Bake for 25 minutes, until the tomatoes are beginning to soften and open up. Sprinkle with oil and basil and serve warm.

whole roast monkfish

Most other fish would be overwhelmed by the robust flavours in this Provençal dish, which is ideal for those who are not great lovers of fish. Make sure the thin grey membrane that lies under the skin is removed.

1 monkfish tail, about 600 g/1 lb 5 oz.

about 12 thin slices smoked bacon or pancetta – enough to cover the fish

2 tablespoons extra virgin olive oil

200 g/7 oz. mushrooms, sliced

2 large garlic cloves, crushed

250 ml/1 cup dry white wine

1 kg/2 lb 4 oz. tomatoes, skinned, deseeded and chopped

2 tablespoons crème fraîche/sour cream

a handful of fresh basil leaves, chopped

coarse sea salt and freshly ground black pepper

Serves 4

Preheat the oven to 220°C (425°F) Gas 7. Place the bacon on a work surface with the slices slightly overlapping each other. Put the monkfish on top, belly side up. Wrap it in the bacon with the ends overlapping across the belly. Turn it over and set aside.

Heat the oil in a large frying pan/skillet. Add the mushrooms and a pinch of salt and cook until browned, 3–5 minutes. Stir in the garlic, then add the wine and cook over high heat for 1 minute. Stir in the tomatoes, salt lightly and simmer gently for 5 minutes.

Pour this tomato sauce into a baking dish just large enough to hold the fish. Set the fish on top and roast for 15 minutes. Lower the temperature to 200°C (400°F) Gas 6 and roast for 30 minutes more. Remove from the oven and put the fish on a plate. Stir the crème fraîche/sour cream and basil into the sauce. Place the monkfish back on top and serve.

easy fish stew

This easy, stress-free fish stew makes a fantastic dish for dinner. Don't forget to provide a few empty dishes for discarded shells and some bowls of warm water for washing fingers.

5 tablespoons olive oil

3 garlic cloves, crushed and chopped

2 onions, chopped

2 leeks, trimmed and sliced

3 celery stalks, sliced

1 fennel bulb, trimmed and sliced

1 tablespoon plain/all-purpose flour

1 bay leaf

a sprig of fresh thyme

a generous pinch of saffron threads

3 x 400-g/14-oz. cans chopped tomatoes

2 litres/8 cups fish stock

1 kg/2 lb 4 oz. monkfish tail, cut into 8 pieces

500 g/1 lb 2 oz. mussels in shells, scrubbed

8 scallops

8 uncooked prawns/shrimp, shell on

a bunch of fresh flat-leaf parsley, chopped

sea salt and freshly ground black pepper

warm crusty bread, to serve

Serves 8

Heat the oil in a large saucepan and add the garlic, onions, leeks, celery and fennel. Cook over low to medium heat for 10 minutes, until soft. Sprinkle in the flour and stir well. Add the bay leaf, thyme, saffron, tomatoes, fish stock and season with salt and pepper to taste. Bring to the boil, then simmer for 25 minutes. Add the monkfish, mussels, scallops and prawns/shrimp, cover with a lid and simmer very gently for 6 minutes. Remove from the heat and set aside, with the lid on, for 4 minutes. Add the parsley and serve with plenty of warm crusty bread.

Spanish clams *with ham*

In the Mediterranean, clams usually go straight into the cooking pot with oil and garlic. Herbs and a splash of wine are often added. Since Spanish cured hams are of such exceptional quality, adding even a little will season and enliven many savoury dishes. 'Mar i montaña' (sea and mountains) is a typically Catalan cooking idea that has spread worldwide. Catalans revel in unusual combinations, such as cooking game with chocolate, juniper or cinnamon, or adding saffron to both sweet and savoury dishes.

2 tablespoons extra virgin olive oil

500 g/1 lb 2 oz. live clams in the shell, or frozen raw clams, thawed

50 g/1¾ oz. jamón serrano or Parma ham, cut into thin strips

1 small green chilli/chile, deseeded and chopped

2 garlic cloves, sliced

4 tablespoons white wine or cider

2 tablespoons chopped spring onion/scallion tops, fresh chives or flat-leaf parsley

Serves 4

Put the olive oil, clams, ham, chilli/chile and garlic in a flameproof casserole dish and stir over high heat. When the clams begin to open, add the wine, cover and tilt the pan a few times to mix the ingredients. Cook on high for 2–3 minutes, or until all the clams have opened. Discard any that do not open.

Sprinkle with the spring onions/scallions or herbs. Cover again for 1 minute, then serve in shallow bowls.

lemon and herb chicken
with roasted vegetables

a handful each of fresh coriander/cilantro, mint and flat-leaf parsley leaves

2 garlic cloves

3 small red chillies/chiles, deseeded

½ teaspoon ground cumin

1 tablespoon chopped preserved lemon peel

4 tablespoons olive oil

6 chicken thigh fillets, halved

1 medium aubergine/eggplant, cut into large cubes

2 courgettes/zucchini, thickly sliced

1 small red bell pepper, quartered and deseeded

1 red onion, cut into thin wedges

2 tablespoons freshly squeezed lemon juice

sea salt and freshly ground black pepper

lemon wedges, to serve

Serves 4

This is a deliciously lemony dish with a hint of heat, perfect for feeding a crowd on a warm evening. It is also delicious eaten cold, so can be served for lunch the following day or, when sliced, it makes a good sandwich filling served in rustic bread with some mayonnaise and rocket/arugula.

Preheat the oven to 220°C (425°F) Gas 7.

Put the herbs, garlic, chillies/chiles, cumin, preserved lemon, 1 tablespoon of the oil and a little salt and pepper in a food processor and process until finely chopped. Put the chicken in a non-metallic bowl, add the herb mixture and toss to coat the chicken. Cover and refrigerate while you cook the vegetables.

Put 2 tablespoons of the oil in a roasting pan and put it in the oven for 10 minutes to heat up.

Put the aubergine/eggplant, courgettes/ zucchini, red bell pepper and onion in the hot roasting pan and season well with salt and pepper. Cook in the oven for 40 minutes, shaking the pan and turning the vegetables

after about 20 minutes. Remove from the oven and cover with kitchen foil to keep warm while you cook the chicken.

Heat the remaining oil in a frying pan/skillet set over medium heat. Put the chicken in the pan and reserve the marinade in the bowl. Cook the chicken for 7–8 minutes, until a golden crust forms, spooning the reserved marinade over the top. Turn over and cook for 5 minutes, until cooked through. Pour the lemon juice over the chicken and turn the chicken over in the pan.

Arrange the vegetables and chicken on a serving dish. Serve with couscous or rice, if liked, and lemon wedges for squeezing.

Greek chicken stifado

In Greece, stifado (or stifatho) can refer to a number of things, but essentially it is a thickened stew with tomato, garlic and olive oil – perfect for summer. Sometimes made with beef or rabbit, guinea fowl or even quail, it is a handsome dish, easy to prepare, and fragrant with herbs. The flambé is an unusual touch – it's entirely optional, but fun, especially with a pleasant, fruity Metaxa brandy. Serve straight from the dish, accompanied with torn country bread, noodles or rice. Oddly, it's even sometimes served with chips/French fries.

1.5 kg/3 lb 5 oz. chicken, whole or quartered, or 4 breast or leg portions

2 tablespoons extra virgin olive oil

10 whole cloves

20 pearl onions or 10 shallots, halved

8 canned artichokes, drained

4 garlic cloves, chopped

2 tablespoons white wine vinegar or lemon juice

6 tablespoons rich tomato purée/paste (double strength)

450 g/1 lb. canned chopped tomatoes

24 black olives, such as Kalamata

a large bunch fresh or dried rosemary, oregano, thyme, or a mixture

2 tablespoons Greek Metaxa brandy (optional)

freshly ground black pepper

Serves 4

Pat the chicken dry with paper towels. Heat the olive oil in a large flameproof casserole dish, add the chicken and sauté for 8–10 minutes, turning it with tongs occasionally.

Push the cloves into some of the pearl onions and add them all to the pan. Add the artichokes, garlic, vinegar, tomato purée/paste, canned tomatoes, olives and freshly ground black pepper. Tuck in the herb sprigs.

Bring to the boil and reduce the heat to low. Cover and simmer for 30 minutes for chicken pieces, or about 60 minutes if using a whole bird, until the chicken is tender and the sauce has reduced and thickened.

Heat the brandy in a warmed ladle and pour it, flaming, over the stifado. Serve immediately.

steak *with blue cheese butter*

Fillet steak topped with melting blue cheese, walnuts and herbs: simple, impressive and irresistible. Serve with a salad of baby spinach leaves for the perfect summer evening treat.

4 x 200-g/7-oz. fillet steaks
sea salt and freshly ground black pepper
baby spinach salad, to serve

BLUE CHEESE BUTTER
50 g/3½ tablespoons butter, softened
50 g/1¾ oz. soft blue cheese, such as Gorgonzola
25 g/¼ cup walnuts, finely ground in a blender
2 tablespoons chopped fresh flat-leaf parsley
sea salt and freshly ground black pepper

Serves 4

To make the blue cheese butter, put the butter, cheese, walnuts and parsley into a bowl and beat well. Season to taste. Form into a log, wrap in kitchen foil and chill for about 30 minutes.

Lightly season the steaks and cook on a preheated barbecue (or pan-fry in a very hot pan in a little oil) for 3 minutes on each side for rare, or 4–5 minutes for medium to well done.

Cut the butter into 8 slices. Put 2 slices of butter onto each steak, wrap loosely with foil and let rest for 5 minutes. Serve the steaks with a salad of baby spinach.

pork fillet *with Marsala*

This recipe, which is based on the more common veal escalopes with Marsala, is easy to make with pork fillets (also called tenderloins) cut into small oval escalopes or scaloppine. Serve with side dishes such as buttered spinach or tiny roasted potatoes, and a soft red wine, a glass of the same sweet Marsala used in the sauce, or a dry Marsala.

1½–2 pork tenderloins, about 750 g/1 lb 10 oz.
100 g/¾ cup plain/all-purpose flour
1 teaspoon salt
1 teaspoon ground ginger or grated nutmeg
50 g/3½ tablespoons salted butter
2 tablespoons extra virgin olive oil
25 g/1 oz. blanched almonds, flaked or whole
100 ml/⅓ cup sweet Marsala wine
2 tablespoons jellied veal or beef stock, or canned beef or chicken consommé

Serves 4

Cut the tenderloins crossways into 1-cm/ ½-inch slices. Cut each slice almost through again, then open out and press flat with the heel of your palm. You should have about 24 flattened, butterflied pieces or scaloppine.

Sift the flour, salt and ginger together onto a flat plate. Press the pieces of pork into this mixture until well coated on both sides. Put half the butter and half the oil in a non-stick frying pan/skillet and heat until sizzling. Cook

the almonds briefly until golden, then remove with a slotted spoon and set aside. Add 6 prepared scaloppine to the pan and cook for 2 minutes on each side, pressing them down well, then remove with tongs and keep hot. Continue with a second batch of 6.

Add half the Marsala to the pan and stir to dissolve the sediment. Pour off into a bowl and keep it warm. Wash and dry the pan. Using the remaining butter and oil, repeat the process until the second batch of pork is cooked. Keep hot in the same way.

Pour the remaining Marsala into the pan, then add the jellied meat stock or consommé. Scrape, stir and heat until well dissolved, then add the reserved warm pan sauce made earlier. Heat again until sticky and intensely flavoured. Return the pork to the pan and turn it in the hot sauce. Serve 6 scaloppine per person, with a generous spoonful of the rich, sticky Marsala glaze and the nuts.

Sicilian-style lamb cutlets
with lemon and garlic marinade

When it comes to meat, Sicily is synonymous with lamb, especially in spring. In Palermo at Easter, the locals often roast a leg of lamb in the forests near the city. If you are lucky enough to be there, you'll notice the smoke wafting in every direction, and the air heavy with the scent of roasting lamb – wonderful inspiration for this delicious dish.

1 kg/2 lb 4 oz. lamb cutlets
6 garlic cloves, crushed
freshly squeezed juice of 2 lemons
5 tablespoons extra virgin olive oil
1 teaspoon dried oregano
1 bay leaf, torn
freshly ground black pepper

TO SERVE
100 g/3½ oz. wild rocket/arugula
coarse sea salt
lemon wedges

Serves 4–6

Put the lamb cutlets in a freezer bag, then add the garlic, lemon juice, olive oil, oregano, bay leaf and plenty of black pepper. Seal tightly and let stand for 1–24 hours, turning occasionally. (If marinating for more than 1 hour, put the meat in the refrigerator.)

Drain the cutlets, reserving the marinade. Put them on a preheated hot barbecue, under a preheated grill or on a hot stove-top grill pan, and cook for 20–30 minutes, or until golden brown, turning occasionally and basting with the marinade. To check they are cooked, cut into the thickest part with a sharp knife – if still pink, cook for an extra 10 minutes. Alternatively, put the cutlets in a roasting pan with 100 ml/⅓ cup cold water and cook in a preheated oven at 180°C (350°F) Gas 4 for 60 minutes, turning once. Reserve the pan juices to pour over the lamb when serving.

Spread the rocket/arugula over a serving dish, place the cutlets on top, sprinkle with salt and serve with lemon wedges.

Sisteron-style roast lamb

The town of Sisteron in Haute-Provence has been known since Roman times as the gateway to Provence. Sheep dot the high pastures nearby, nibbling the wild mountain herbs. A famous local breed is the Préalpes, which has a long head, spindly legs and sparse wool. The quality of its meat is exceptional: tender and tasty.

650 g/1 lb 7 oz. large baking potatoes, peeled

a handful of fresh thyme, rosemary or marjoram

4 garlic cloves, peeled and sliced

3–4 tablespoons extra virgin olive oil

1 leg of lamb, ideally from a herb-fed mountain breed, about 2–2.2 kg/4½–5 lbs

200 ml/¾ cup lamb stock or water

1 x 50-g/1¾-oz. can anchovy fillets

1 small handful of fresh flat-leaf parsley, snipped with scissors

freshly ground sea salt and black pepper

Serves 4–6

Preheat the oven to 220°C (425°F) Gas 7. Cut the potatoes into 5-mm/½-inch slices. Arrange them in overlapping lines or circles in a roasting pan or ovenproof dish. Put half the herb sprigs into the centre of the potatoes. Strip the leaves from the rest, place in a mortar with the garlic and pound to a pulp. Add a tablespoon of the olive oil and mix again. Rub this mixture all over the lamb, then place it on top of the potatoes.

Mix the remaining oil with the stock or water and pour it over the lamb. Drizzle the oil from the anchovy can all over the potatoes, and dot the fillets on top.

Roast, uncovered, for 30 minutes. Reduce the temperature to 160°C (325°F) Gas 3 and continue to cook for another hour, or until the lamb is golden outside and pink at the bone. A meat thermometer should read 65–70°C (150–160°F). Let rest for 10 minutes, then scatter over the parsley.

Slice the lamb thickly and serve hot with the potatoes.

desserts & drinks

200 ml/¾ cup double/heavy cream

200 ml/¾ cup milk

75 g/⅓ cup caster/superfine sugar

2 tablespoons Galliano liqueur or
1 teaspoon vanilla extract

2 tablespoons boiling water

1 tablespoon powdered gelatine

SUMMER FRUIT COMPOTE

150 g/1½ cups blueberries (optional)

50–75 g/1¾–2¾ oz. granulated sugar

100 g/¾ cup raspberries or loganberries

100 g/¾ cup small strawberries

4 ramekins

Serves 4

Put the cream and milk in a small saucepan, simmer gently for 5 minutes over low heat, then add the sugar and the Galliano.

Pour the boiling water into a small heatproof dish and sprinkle the gelatine over the surface (make sure that the tablespoon is level). Leave to stand for a few seconds until the gelatine absorbs the water. Stir until the gelatine has dissolved, then add it to the cream mixture, stirring well. Pour the cream mixture through a sieve/strainer into a jug/pitcher, pushing any bits through the sieve/strainer with the back of a wooden spoon. Pour the mixture into 4 ramekins and chill overnight or until set.

To make the summer fruit compote, put the blueberries in a saucepan, if using, with 50 g/¼ cup of the sugar and 2 tablespoons of water. Set over low heat and cook until the juices start to run. Add the raspberries and strawberries, stir carefully, turn off the heat and leave to cool. Taste and add extra sugar, if necessary, then cover and chill until required.

When ready to serve, dip the ramekins of pannacotta quickly in shallow boiling water, then invert onto 4 serving plates. Holding the plate and ramekin together, give it a firm shake, then turn out the pannacotta carefully onto each plate. It should be quite wobbly and will plop out of the ramekin onto the plate. Add a spoonful of compote, then serve.

pannacotta Galliano
with summer fruit compote

Pannacotta, literally 'cooked cream', is flavoured with vanilla in its classic form, but Galliano (a golden, vanilla-flavoured Italian liqueur), makes a lovely addition. The creamy just-set texture of the pannacotta with berries makes a pleasing change from the usual cream or custard. You could try adding shavings of dark/bittersweet chocolate instead.

nectarines in sambuca and lime juice

Sambuca is a sweet Italian liqueur made from elderflowers, which was popularized when Italian restaurants took to serving it with a flaming coffee bean on top. It is suited to summer fruits, and if you are lucky enough to live in an area where elders grow, you can scatter the delicate flowers over the fruit just before serving.

8 ripe nectarines
3 tablespoons caster/superfine sugar
2 tablespoons sambuca
finely grated zest and freshly squeezed juice of 1 lime
lime wedges, to serve

Serves 4

Slice the nectarines thinly (discard the stones/pits) and put in a bowl. Add the sugar, sambuca and lime juice, cover and leave for 2 hours to marinate, if possible. When ready to serve, transfer to serving bowls, then sprinkle with the lime zest and serve with lime wedges.

fresh figs *with Vin Santo and mascarpone*

This lovely, simple dish is best served when you can find very good quality fresh figs, preferably straight from the tree. Vin Santo is an Italian sweet wine that marries well with the flavour of both the figs and the mascarpone – if you can't find it, you could also use port or a cream sherry.

250 g/generous 1 cup mascarpone cheese
25–50 g/scant ¼–½ cup icing/confectioners' sugar, or to taste
6 tablespoons Vin Santo, plus extra to serve
12 ripe figs

Serves 6

Put the mascarpone into a bowl, add the icing/confectioners' sugar and Vin Santo and beat until smooth. Set aside to infuse for 30 minutes, then transfer to a small serving bowl. Cut the figs in half and arrange on a large serving platter with the bowl of mascarpone.

fruit platter

Everyone loves fruit, especially if it's all been prepared for them and looks stunning. This one is always a winner.

1 ripe melon, such as orange cantaloupe or green honeydew
2 papayas
juice of 2 limes
300 g/2½ cups mixed berries, such as blackberries, blueberries, raspberries, redcurrants and strawberries

HONEY YOGURT
450 ml/1¾ cups plain Greek-style yogurt
6 tablespoons clear honey

Serves 4

Peel, halve and deseed the melon, then cut into wedges and slice. Divide between 4 plates. Peel, halve, deseed and cut the papaya into wedges. Add to the melon. Sprinkle with lime juice, then add the berries.

Put the yogurt in a bowl, drizzle with the honey and serve with the fruit.

spiced muscat figs

Muscat is a grape variety that produces deliciously sweet and syrupy dessert wines known as moscato in Italy and moscatel in Spain. Whichever one you choose, the result will be the same: a deliciously fragrant and light dessert that will wow your guests.

Put the muscat, sugar, vanilla, cardamom pods and orange zest in a medium saucepan and set over high heat. Bring the mixture to the boil, then reduce the heat to medium. Add the figs to the pan, cover and cook for 20–25 minutes, until the figs are very tender. Remove the figs from the pan with a slotted spoon and set aside.

Return the liquid to the boil and cook for 8–10 minutes, until thick and syrupy.

Serve 2 figs per person, with the syrup spooned over the top.

250 ml/1 cup muscat (sweet dessert wine)
125 g/⅔ cup granulated sugar
1 vanilla bean
2 cardamom pods, lightly crushed
2 strips of orange zest
8 fresh green figs

Serves 4

berries *with honeyed yogurt*

200 g/2 cups fresh mixed red berries
a strip of lemon zest
a squeeze of lemon juice
a pinch of ground cinnamon
500 ml/2 cups plain Greek-style yogurt
6 tablespoons clear honey

Serves 4–6

Reserve a few of the most attractive berries to garnish and put the remainder in a saucepan. Add the lemon zest, lemon juice, cinnamon and 1 tablespoon water. Heat gently for about 3 minutes until the berries just start to soften slightly. Let cool, then spoon them into glasses. Add the yogurt and honey. Top with the reserved berries and serve immediately.

Yogurt is remarkably refreshing on a warm day, especially when served with tart summer berries. This dessert is simplicity itself to prepare and the berries are given a little extra lift with a pinch of cinnamon and some sticky honey. A thick Greek-style yogurt is best, but any plain yogurt can be used. A dash of orange-flavoured liqueur, such as Cointreau, can be added to the berries, if liked.

affogato parfait

An affogato is a popular Italian dessert: vanilla ice cream doused in a shot of hot espresso and sometimes a sweet liqueur such as Frangelico, Amaretto or Strega. Here, all the flavour of an affogato is captured in a parfait log, which can be served with a little glass of liqueur on the side.

125 ml/½ cup strong black espresso coffee
150 g/¾ cup granulated sugar
1 vanilla bean
5 egg yolks
3 tablespoons Frangelico or grappa
500 ml/2 cups crème fraîche/sour cream
250 ml/1 cup double/heavy cream
100 g/⅔ cup hazelnuts, lightly toasted and roughly chopped

a loaf pan, 8 x 22 cm/3¼ x 8½ inches, lined with plastic wrap

Serves 6–8

Put the coffee and sugar in a small saucepan and set over high heat. Rub the vanilla bean between your palms to soften it, then use a sharp knife to split it open lengthways. Scrape the seeds directly into the saucepan. Bring the mixture to the boil, then reduce the heat to medium and let the liquid simmer for 10 minutes, stirring occasionally, until syrupy. Remove from the heat.

Put the egg yolks in a large bowl and use a balloon whisk to beat until thick and pale.

Add the warm coffee syrup. Beat until well combined, then add the Frangelico. Add the crème fraîche/sour cream and double/heavy cream and beat until well combined. Pour into the prepared loaf pan and freeze overnight.

Remove the parfait from the freezer and let it sit for a few minutes before carefully turning out onto a chilled serving platter. Sprinkle with the hazelnuts and slice into individual portions to serve with a little glass of whatever Italian liqueur you fancy on the side.

summer fruit compote
with zabaglione

Zabaglione is another classic Italian dessert that combines a few simple ingredients to stunning effect. It needs to be made at the very last minute, so it will keep you in the kitchen for a short while, but it is well worth the effort. Strawberries, peaches and nectarines are used here, as they taste and look so good together, but any combination of your favourite summer fruits will work. Small glasses of a floral dessert wine would be great served with this.

220 g/generous 1 cup granulated sugar
2 nectarines, pitted and cut into thick wedges
2 peaches, pitted and cut into thick wedges
500 g/4 cups fresh strawberries, hulled

ZABAGLIONE
4 egg yolks
60 g/⅓ cup caster/superfine sugar
100 ml/⅓ cup Marsala or sweet sherry

Serves 4–6

Put the granulated sugar in a large saucepan with 750 ml/3 cups water and set over high heat. Bring to the boil and boil for 5 minutes. Remove from the heat and let cool completely.

Put the fruit in a non-reactive bowl and pour the cooled syrup over the top. Cover and chill for 3–6 hours.

To make the zabaglione, put the egg yolks, caster/superfine sugar and Marsala in a large heatproof bowl. Set the bowl over a saucepan of barely simmering water, making sure the bottom of the bowl does not come into contact with the water. Use a balloon whisk or hand-held electric whisk to beat gently for a few minutes, until well combined, then beat more vigorously for about 8–10 minutes, until the mixture has doubled in volume and is thick and spoonable.

Use a slotted spoon to transfer the fruit to a serving platter and spoon the warm zabaglione over the top. Serve immediately.

messy strawberries Romanoff

This is a foolproof dessert that pays homage to a popular fine-dining dish from the 1970s. Ready-made meringues are roughly broken and arranged on a serving platter, then topped with whipped cream and Cointreau-macerated ripe summer strawberries.

500 g/4 cups fresh strawberries, hulled
65 ml/¼ cup Cointreau or other orange-flavoured liqueur
6 ready-made meringues
125 ml/½ cup whipping/heavy cream
4 tablespoons icing/confectioners' sugar, plus extra for dusting

Serves 4

Put the strawberries in a non-reactive bowl and add the Cointreau. Cover and let sit at room temperature for 3 hours, stirring often. Roughly break each meringue into 3–4 pieces and put them on a serving platter.

Put the cream in a grease-free bowl and use a balloon whisk or hand-held electric whisk to whip. Add the icing/confectioners' sugar a little at a time as you whip, until the mixture forms soft peaks.

Spoon the cream over the meringue, then arrange the strawberries on top, along with a tablespoon or two of the juice. Dust with icing/confectioners' sugar just before serving.

VARIATION
Try replacing the strawberries with raspberries or blackberries or even sliced poached peaches, scattered with toasted flaked almonds.

2 egg yolks
6 tablespoons Marsala wine
5 tablespoons caster/superfine sugar
150 g/5½ oz. dark/bittersweet chocolate
(over 60 per cent cocoa solids)
250 g/1 cup mascarpone cheese
2 tablespoons dark rum
300 ml/1¼ cups double/heavy cream
100 ml/⅓ cup Italian espresso coffee
24 savoiardi biscuits/ladyfingers

Serves 4–6

To make the zabaglione, put the egg yolks, 2 tablespoons of the Marsala and 2 tablespoons of the sugar in a medium heatproof bowl and beat with a hand-held electric mixer or balloon whisk until well blended. Set over a saucepan of gently simmering water (the bottom should at no time be in contact with the water). Do not let the water boil.

Whisk the mixture until it is glossy, pale, light and fluffy and holds a trail when dropped from the whisk, about 5 minutes. Remove from the heat and whisk until cold.

Put the chocolate in a blender or food processor and grind to a powder. Set aside. Put the mascarpone and remaining sugar in a bowl and beat well, then beat in another 2 tablespoons Marsala and the rum. Gently fold into the zabaglione.

Whisk the cream until soft peaks form, then fold into the zabaglione mixture. Mix the espresso and remaining Marsala in a bowl. Dip the savoiardi/ladyfingers into the espresso mixture one at a time – don't leave them in for too long or they will disintegrate. Start assembling the tiramisù by setting half the dipped fingers in the bottom of a serving dish or 4–6 glasses. Sprinkle with any leftover coffee. Sprinkle with one-third of the pulverized chocolate. Spoon over half the mascarpone mixture, arrange the remaining fingers on top, moisten with any remaining coffee and sprinkle with half the remaining chocolate. Finally, spoon over the remaining mascarpone mixture and finish with a thick layer of chocolate. Chill in the fridge for at last 3 hours (overnight is better) for the flavours to develop. Serve chilled.

tiramisù

Tiramisù is said to have originated in Venice in the 1950s. For added texture, pulverize real chocolate in a blender for layering and sprinkling. This recipe goes easy on the sugar, but you can add more to the cream mixture if you like. Make in a large glass dish or in small glasses for a special occasion.

strawberry tiramisù

This is a slight adaptation of a fantastic recipe from Italian cookery writer Valentina Harris. It is a wonderful variation on the classic dessert.

400 g/3⅓ cups fresh ripe strawberries
5 hard amaretti biscuits/cookies
2 large eggs, separated
40 g/scant ¼ cup caster/superfine sugar
¼ teaspoon vanilla extract
4 tablespoons white rum
250 g/1 cup mascarpone cheese, at room temperature
3 tablespoons whipping/heavy cream
100 ml/⅓ cup pressed apple juice
100 g/3½ oz. savoiardi biscuits/ladyfingers

a medium–large, deep glass dessert bowl

Serves 6

Cut the stalks off the strawberries. Weigh 100 g/¾ cup and chop them finely. Slice the remaining strawberries and set aside. Put the amaretti biscuits/cookies in a plastic bag, seal, then hit them with a rolling pin until they are the consistency of coarse breadcrumbs.

Beat the egg yolks in a bowl with an electric hand-held whisk or a balloon whisk until pale yellow and fluffy, gradually adding the sugar. Add the vanilla extract and a tablespoon of the white rum. Tip the mascarpone into a large bowl, beat with a wooden spoon to soften, then gradually add the egg yolk mixture and beat until smooth. In another bowl, whisk the egg whites until they just hold a soft peak. Fold the chopped strawberries into the mascarpone mixture, then carefully fold in the egg whites.

Whip the whipping/heavy cream to a similar consistency, then fold that in too, together

with a third of the crushed amaretti biscuits/cookies. Mix the remaining rum with the apple juice. Dip some of the savoiardi/ladyfingers in the apple-rum mixture and lay across the base of the bowl. Reserving some for decoration, arrange a layer of sliced strawberries over the fingers, then cover with a layer of mascarpone cream. Repeat with 1 or 2 more layers of soaked fingers, strawberries and mascarpone

cream, finishing with the mascarpone cream. Cover the bowl tightly with plastic wrap and chill in the fridge for at least 5 hours.

About 1 hour before serving, sprinkle the remaining amaretti over the top of the tiramisù, then decorate with the remaining strawberries. Return the tiramisù to the fridge until you are ready to serve it.

grape and lemon mascarpone tart

This is a really simple dessert that you can make with a ready-rolled pastry base. A gorgeous Italian lemon liqueur gives a sharp edge to the creamy mascarpone.

230 g/8 oz. ready-rolled puff pastry dough, thawed if frozen

2 large eggs, separated

2 tablespoons caster/superfine sugar, plus 1 teaspoon for sprinkling

250 g/1 cup mascarpone cheese

2½ tablespoons Limoncello (lemon liqueur)

250 g/2½ cups white seedless or halved and seeded grapes, rinsed and dried

250 g/2½ cups red seedless or halved and seeded grapes, rinsed and dried

1 teaspoon icing/confectioners' sugar

a large square or rectangular baking sheet, lightly greased

Serves 6–8

Preheat the oven to 200°C (400°F) Gas 6. Take the pastry out of the fridge and let it rest for 20 minutes. Unroll and lift carefully onto the baking sheet. Trim around the edge to make a 28-cm/11¼-inch round.

Lightly whisk the egg whites and brush a thin layer onto the pastry. Sprinkle with 1 teaspoon caster/superfine sugar, then use a fork to prick the pastry all over. Bake for 10–12 minutes until puffy and brown. Let cool.

Tip the mascarpone into a bowl and gradually work in the Limoncello. Using an electric hand-held whisk, beat the egg yolks with the remaining caster/superfine sugar until pale, thick and creamy. Gently fold the mascarpone mixture into the eggs until thoroughly blended.

Transfer the cooled pastry base to a large serving plate or tray. Spread over the mascarpone mixture with a spatula, taking it almost up to the edges. Scatter the grapes on top to get a nice mix of colours. Serve straight away or chill for a couple of hours. Sprinkle with icing/confectioners' sugar immediately before serving.

Napoléons *with lemon cream and strawberries*

Traditionally, Napoléons (also called millefeuilles or 'thousand leaves') are rectangles of puff pastry alternating with layers of pastry cream, topped with marbled fondant icing. This recipe is a departure from tradition, with a more interesting combination of flavours (and is much prettier too).

500 g/1 lb 2 oz. puff pastry dough
milk, for brushing
caster/superfine sugar, for sprinkling
800 g/6½ cups strawberries, thinly sliced
icing/confectioners' sugar, to serve

LEMON CREAM
2 large whole eggs and 3 egg yolks
6 tablespoons granulated sugar
freshly squeezed juice of 3 lemons, strained
100 g/7 tablespoons unsalted butter, cut into pieces
125 ml/½ cup whipping/heavy cream, chilled

a baking sheet, lined with parchment paper

Serves 4–5

Roll out the pastry dough to a large square just under 1.5 cm/¾ inch thick. Cut out 10 rectangles about 7 x 13 cm/2¾ x 5¼ inches. Preheat the oven to 200°C (400°F) Gas 6.

Arrange the rectangles on the lined baking sheet. Brush with milk and sprinkle with sugar. Bake until puffed and golden, 10–15 minutes. When cool, carefully cut each one in half horizontally, using a serrated knife, to obtain 2 thin layers.

To make the lemon cream, mix the eggs, egg yolks and sugar in a saucepan. Add the lemon juice and whisk lightly. Add the butter and cook over low heat, stirring constantly until thick. Remove from the heat, transfer to a bowl and let cool. (The recipe can be made up to 1 day in advance up to this point.)

No more than a few hours before serving, whip the cream until it holds stiff peaks. Fold into the lemon mixture until blended. Set aside.

To assemble the Napoléons, set one pastry bottom slice on a tray. Spread with a spoonful of lemon cream, then top with a single layer of strawberry slices. Add another pastry layer and repeat. Add a top pastry layer (one of the more puffed and golden ones). Repeat until all the layers have been used. You won't always be able to have a bottom pastry layer on the bottom, which is fine, but you do need a top layer on top. Refrigerate until needed (no more than 6–8 hours).

Dust with icing/confectioners' sugar before serving, allowing 1–2 Napoléons per person.

fresh fruit tart

In French patisseries, this tart is often made in an orderly fashion, with all the fruit arranged in neat circles. It is prettier – and more accessible for the home cook – to use the higgledy-piggledy approach to fruit distribution. You can pile it as high as you like, but be warned that it can get a bit messy when serving.

500 g/2 cups ready-made pastry cream (crème pâtissière) or custard
1 ready-made baked sweet pastry case/shell

FRUIT FILLING
125 g/1 cup blackberries
100 g/1 cup blueberries
125 g/1 cup strawberries
1 peach, thinly sliced
1 nectarine, thinly sliced
2 purple plums, thinly sliced
1 kiwifruit, peeled, halved and thinly sliced
about 150 g/½ cup apricot jam/jelly

Serves 8–10

Spread the pastry cream in an even layer in the tart case/shell. Arrange the fruit on top. Start with one kind, using almost all of it, and then go on to another, until you have used all the types. Then go back and fill in the holes with the remaining pieces.

Melt the jam/jelly and 2 tablespoons water in a small saucepan over low heat. Strain to remove all the lumps. Using a pastry brush, carefully but generously dab or brush the jam/jelly over the fruit to form a shiny glaze. Let cool. Refrigerate 6–8 hours in advance, but return almost to room temperature to serve.

VARIATION
For a fresh strawberry tart, use 300–400 g/2½–3¼ cups washed and dried strawberries, halved and/or sliced, depending on size. Glaze with redcurrant jelly instead of apricot jam/jelly – it shouldn't need straining.

strawberry tart

When any fruit is abundant and in season, it just has to be used in a tart with sweet and crumbling pastry. This mixture of wild and farmed strawberries is delicious – the tiny wild strawberries look so beautiful and are packed with flavour. If you can't find them, use the same weight of farmed strawberries. Any other soft fruit can be used, just make sure you pile the tart high with fruit.

300 g/scant 2½ cups plain/all-purpose flour
200 g/1¾ sticks butter, cut into small pieces
150 g/1 cup light brown sugar
2–3 egg yolks, beaten
200 g/⅔ cup redcurrant jelly
250 g/2 cups wild strawberries
750 g/6 cups farmed strawberries, hulled
double/heavy cream or plain yogurt mixed with honey, to serve

a non-stick flan pan, 30 cm/12 inches diameter

Serves 8

Put the flour into a mixing bowl and add the butter. Using your fingertips, rub the butter into the flour until it looks like breadcrumbs. Add the sugar and mix. Make a well in the middle and add 2 of the egg yolks. Mix with a round-bladed knife, using cutting motions, until the mixture forms a ball, adding an extra egg yolk if needed. Dust your hands lightly with flour, bring the mixture together and transfer to a lightly floured, cool surface.

Roll out the pastry to just bigger than the pan. Line the pan with the pastry, prick all over with a fork and chill for 20 minutes. Preheat the oven to 180°C (350°F) Gas 4.

Bake for 20 minutes, then reduce the temperature to 150°C (300°F) Gas 2 and cook for a further 20 minutes. Remove from the oven and let cool, then transfer to a flat serving plate and cover with plastic wrap until needed.

Put the redcurrant jelly into a small saucepan and heat gently until thin and smooth. Remove and let cool a little while you pile the strawberries into the cooked pastry case, cutting any very large berries into smaller pieces. Spoon the redcurrant jelly over the strawberries and serve with double/heavy cream or plain yogurt mixed with honey.

peach and Sauternes ice cream

What do you drink with ice cream? Remembering that your tastebuds become rather frozen into inaction, it's best to choose something strongly flavoured and sweet, such as the Sauternes used in this recipe.

325 ml/1⅓ cups sweet dessert wine, such as Sauternes
200 g/1 cup granulated sugar, or to taste
6 yellow peaches
250 ml/1 cup whipping/heavy cream

TO SERVE
sprigs of fresh mint
1 ripe peach, sliced into wedges

an ice-cream maker

Makes about 1 litre/4 cups

Place the wine in saucepan, add the sugar, heat gently and stir until dissolved. Add the peaches in a single layer and poach them until cooked but not soft. (Turn them over when half cooked if the liquid does not cover them.)

Cool and chill, then slip off the skins, cut in half, and remove the stones/pits. Place the flesh in a blender and purée with enough poaching liquid to make 750 ml/3 cups. Add sugar to taste.

Mix the purée into the whipping/heavy cream. Churn in an ice-cream maker, then transfer to the freezer. Serve, decorated with the sprigs of mint and peach slices, if using.

VARIATION
Poach the peaches as above, substituting water for the sweet wine, and adding an extra 2 tablespoons caster/superfine sugar. Add about 4 tablespoons peach liqueur while churning.

vanilla gelato *with hot cherry sauce*

At last, an ice cream that actually tastes like a real Italian gelato. It has no cream and no eggs, so no making custard. It is silky smooth and heavenly served in a glass dish with delicious warmed Amarena cherries.

1 vanilla bean
1.1 litres/4½ cups whole milk
2 tablespoons dried skimmed milk powder
4 tablespoons cornflour/cornstarch or wheat starch
275 g/1⅓ cups granulated sugar
1 teaspoon vanilla extract
370 g/13 oz. canned Italian Amarena cherries in syrup
2 tablespoons maraschino or kirsch liqueur

an ice-cream maker (optional)

Serves 6

Split the vanilla bean in two lengthways and put in a saucepan with 900 ml/3⅔ cups of the milk. Whisk in the milk powder. Bring to boiling point, turn off the heat and leave to infuse for 20 minutes.

Remove the vanilla bean and scrape out the seeds. Whisk the seeds into the milk. Wash and dry the pod and store in the sugar jar.

Dissolve the cornflour/cornstarch in the remaining milk, then pour into the hot milk and add the sugar. Bring to the boil, stirring constantly, until thickened. Cover the surface with plastic wrap and let cool. Stir in the vanilla extract. Chill, then churn in an ice-cream maker. Alternatively, pour into a shallow tray and freeze until it is frozen around the edges. Mash well with a fork. When it is half-frozen, blend in a food processor until creamy, then cover and freeze until firm. Soften in the fridge for 20 minutes before serving.

To serve, put the cherries, their syrup and the liqueur in a saucepan and heat gently. Serve the ice cream in large scoops with the sauce trickled over it.

300 g/1½ cups granulated sugar
finely grated zest and juice of 6 lemons,
plus 6 medium, even-sized lemons
finely grated zest and juice of
1 orange

an ice-cream maker

Serves 6 (makes about 1 litre/4 cups)

Put the sugar and 600 ml/2⅓ cups water in
a saucepan with the lemon and orange zest.
Bring slowly to the boil and boil rapidly for 3–4
minutes. Remove from the heat and let cool.
Meanwhile, strain the fruit juices into a bowl.
When the syrup is cold, strain it into the juice.
Chill. When cold, churn in an ice-cream maker.

Meanwhile, cut the tops off the remaining
6 lemons and shave a little off each base
so that it will stand up. Scoop out the insides,
squeeze and keep the juice for another time.
Put in the freezer. When the sorbet is frozen,
fill the lemon shells and set the tops back on.
Replace in the freezer until needed. Soften in
the fridge for 10–15 minutes before serving.

lemon sorbet

It's worth making a journey to Italy just to taste lemons that have
been properly ripened in the sun. Walk through a lemon grove when
the glossy green trees are in blossom and the scent is intoxicating. The
beautiful leaves can be used like bay leaves or the more exotic Thai lime
leaves to impart a lemony flavour to sweet and savoury dishes alike.
In this recipe, the addition of some orange zest and juice softens the
acidity of un-sunkissed lemons.

100 g/½ cup caster/superfine sugar
3 egg yolks
3 tablespoons balsamic vinegar
300 ml/1¼ cups double/heavy cream
200 ml/¾ cup whole milk
coarsely ground black pepper, to taste

CRUSHED STRAWBERRIES
400 g/3¼ cups strawberries
1–2 tablespoons caster/superfine sugar
(or to taste)
3 tablespoons strawberry liqueur or crème
de framboise (raspberry-flavoured liqueur)

an ice-cream maker

Serves 4

Put the sugar, egg yolks and vinegar in a heatproof bowl and beat with an electric beater until thick and creamy.

Pour the cream into a saucepan and heat to simmering point. Remove from the heat and stir into the egg mixture. Return to the pan and stir over very low heat until slightly thickened and custard-like. Remove from the heat, pour into a clean bowl and let cool.

When the custard is cold, stir in some coarsely ground black pepper to taste, then transfer to an ice-cream maker and churn until frozen.

About 10 minutes before serving, make the crushed strawberries. Simply mix the strawberries, sugar and liqueur together and crush lightly. Scoop the ice cream into chilled glasses and serve with the crushed strawberries.

balsamic ice cream
with crushed strawberries

Choose a good-quality balsamic vinegar and make sure the black pepper is coarsely ground. If you're not keen on the idea of adding the pepper, the ice cream still tastes pretty good without it, but do try it once. It may seem an unusual combination, but it's delicious.

frothy iced coffee

This light, frothy and refreshing blend is the perfect antidote to a hot summer afternoon. For an extra kick, add a spoonful of Kahlúa.

240 g/8½ oz. crushed ice
120 ml/½ cup whole milk
3 tablespoons freshly brewed espresso
1 tablespoon caster/superfine sugar
a scoop of vanilla ice cream

Serves 1

Put the ice in a blender or liquidizer. Add the milk, espresso and sugar and whizz for about 30 seconds, until frothy and slushy. Pour into a tall glass and top with the ice cream. Serve immediately.

espresso granita

A refreshing end to a meal on a warm summer's day. Good biscotti can be purchased ready-made from deli counters and fine food stores.

Put 4 small glasses or espresso cups in the freezer to chill. Put the sugar and coffee in a cafetière/French press. Add 900 ml/3⅔ cups boiling water and let stand for 5 minutes to develop the flavour. Plunge the cafetière/French press, pour the coffee into a heatproof jug/pitcher and let cool before before chilling in the refrigerator.

When very cold, pour the coffee into a bowl and freeze for about 20 minutes, until ice crystals have formed around the edge. Crush the crystals with a fork and return to the freezer. Repeat this process about 3 times until you have an even mixture of fine ice crystals. Cover and return to the freezer until ready to serve. Serve the granita in the serving glasses or cups with biscotti and a drizzle of cream for anyone who prefers their coffee white.

2 tablespoons granulated sugar
3 tablespoons freshly ground coffee
biscotti, to serve
single/light cream, to serve (optional)

Serves 4

café frappé

Café frappé is real treat – very refreshing, and a great change from regular coffee. You can make it with good instant coffee granules (which gives it a smoother flavour and velvety texture), but if you prefer the flavour of real coffee, make it in the usual way and use 2 tablespoons for this recipe.

900 ml/3⅔ cups whole milk, chilled
100 ml/⅓ cup double/heavy cream, chilled
2 tablespoons instant coffee granules
12 ice cubes

Serves 4

Mix the milk and cream in a jug/pitcher or bowl, then put in the freezer for about 3 hours until frozen. Chill 4 glasses until cold.

Put the instant coffee in a cup with 1 tablespoon boiling water. Stir to dissolve the granules, then cool and chill.

Put the frozen creamy milk, coffee and ice cubes in a blender and whizz until smooth.

Pour into the chilled glasses and serve at once.

VARIATION

If you don't like coffee, try making crushed-ice tea. Simply make a pot of weak tea such as Earl Grey, jasmine, green tea, or one of your favourites. Cool the tea and put it in the freezer. Fork through the tea every 20 minutes to break up the large ice crystals that form. When firm and icy, spoon the mixture into chilled glasses and top with sliced peaches or orange wedges. This also makes an exotic light pudding to finish off an indulgent meal.

To give your frappé a kick, add a dash or two of rich coffee liqueur such as Kahlúa – it's heaven, but for adults only.

white wine spritzer

A pretty spritzer to cool a hot brow.

750 ml/3 cups white wine, chilled
1 litre/4 cups sparkling mineral/soda water, chilled
400 g/4 cups frozen white grapes

Serves 8

Put the chilled white wine, mineral/soda water and frozen grapes in a large jug and mix well. Serve the spritzer in your favourite large glasses.

Note Frozen fruit cubes are great taken on picnics to chill drinks. They do not melt as quickly as ordinary ice cubes and children love eating them too. Try chopping up some orange segments, putting them in ice cube trays, adding fresh orange juice to cover, then freezing.

caipirinha

The caipirinha, along with the equally trendy mojito, whisks its drinker away to warmer climes with its alluring mix of rum and lime. The main difference between them is the use of cachaça, which is made with sugar cane, instead of golden rum.

1 lime
2 brown sugar cubes
crushed ice
3½ tablespoons cachaça

Serves 1

Cut the lime into eighths, squeeze and place in a heavy-based tumbler with the sugar cubes. Crush well with a wooden muddler or pestle. Fill the glass with crushed ice and add the cachaça. Stir vigorously and serve with two short straws.

mojito

Wildly popular in Miami for years, this Cuban concoction can now be found gracing the menus of cocktail bars around the world

5 sprigs of fresh mint
3½ tablespoons golden rum
a squeeze of fresh lime juice
2 dashes of sugar syrup
crushed ice
sparkling mineral/soda water

Serves 1

Put the mint in a tall glass, add the rum, lime juice and sugar syrup. Crush with a long-handled spoon until the aroma of the mint is released. Add some crushed ice and stir vigorously until the mixture and the mint are spread evenly. Top up with soda water and stir again. Serve with two straws.

iced pear sparkle

This unusual sparkling cocktail is very refreshing, and perfect for summer celebrations.

1 teaspoon clear honey
ice cubes
2 tablespoons pear liqueur
2 tablespoons Cointreau, or other orange-flavoured liqueur
¼ pear (nashi if available), peeled and thinly sliced
Champagne or sparkling white wine

Serves 1

Put the honey and some ice in a cocktail shaker and gently crush with a wooden muddler or pestle. Add the pear liqueur and Cointreau, replace the lid and shake briskly but briefly.

Pour into a chilled glass, add some pear slices and top up with Champagne. Serve immediately.

classic sangria

This delicious summer punch is the perfect drink for a balmy evening, especially if you are lucky enough to find yourself sitting by the sea. A large pitcher is the ideal accompaniment for good company, conversation and watching the world go by.

2 oranges, sliced

2 lemons, sliced

1–2 tablespoons caster/superfine sugar, to taste

1.5 litres/6 cups red wine

165 ml/⅔ cup **Grand Marnier** or other orange-flavoured liqueur

1 dessert apple, sliced into thin wedges

ice cubes

clear sparkling lemonade

Serves 12

Place half the orange and lemon slices in a large jug/pitcher and sprinkle over the sugar. Leave to macerate for 15 minutes, then add the wine and Grand Marnier and chill for 1 hour.

When ready to serve, add the apple wedges and remaining orange and lemon slices. Add a few scoops of ice and top up with lemonade to taste. Stir and pour into tall glasses to serve, spooning a little fruit into each, if liked.

peach and strawberry sangria

A fragrant and more delicate version of the classic sangria above. Almost any fruit or liqueur could be added instead – try peach schnapps or crème de framboise (raspberry-flavoured liqueur).

2 fresh peaches, pitted and thinly sliced

250 g/2 cups strawberries, hulled and sliced

1 orange, sliced

150 ml/⅔ cup crème de fraise (strawberry-flavoured liqueur)

1.5 litres/6 cups dry white wine

1 small cucumber, peeled, deseeded and thinly sliced

ice cubes

clear sparkling lemonade

borage flowers, to garnish (optional)

Serves 12

Put the peaches, strawberries and orange slices in a large jug/pitcher with the strawberry-flavoured liqueur. Pour in the wine and chill for 30 minutes. When ready to serve, add the cucumber and some ice and top up with lemonade. Pour into glasses and garnish each serving with borage flowers, if using.

white sangria

This light and refreshing variation
is perfect for those who aren't
keen on red wine.

Put the white wine, orange juice, sugar, fruit
and gin in a large jug/pitcher and refrigerate
for 3 hours, until well chilled, stirring frequently
so that the sugar dissolves.

Put the ice cubes in a large serving jug/pitcher
and pour over the sangria. Serve immediately.

750 ml/3 cups dry white wine

125 ml/½ cup freshly
squeezed orange juice

2 tablespoons caster/
superfine sugar

2 oranges, peeled and white
pith removed, thinly sliced

125 g/1 cup strawberries,
hulled and halved

125 ml/½ cup dry gin

ice cubes, to serve

Serves 4–6

watermelon vodka

This tastes and looks heavenly, but has the effect of dynamite! If you can't get seedless watermelon, just use regular and deseed it.

1 seedless watermelon, chilled
750 ml/3 cups vodka, chilled
lime wedges and ice, to serve

Serves 20

Cut the watermelon in half and scoop out all the flesh. Put into a blender and process until smooth. Remove to a large jug/pitcher, add the vodka and let chill for 2 hours before serving. Alternatively, add sparkling mineral/soda water, or lemonade for those with a sweet tooth. Serve with lime wedges and ice.

elderflower and berry cup

The berry ice cubes give this drink a pretty party feel. Make it in a large pitcher and let it sit for 10 minutes before serving – that way the ice cubes begin to melt, colouring the drink a delicate pink with the berry juices.

150 g/1¼ cups mixed berries, such as raspberries, strawberries and blueberries
120 ml/½ cup elderflower cordial
sparkling mineral/soda water, to top up
elderflowers, to garnish (optional)

an ice cube tray

Serves 4

Divide the berries between the ice cube tray holes and top up with still water. Freeze for 2 hours, or until frozen.

Unmould the ice cubes into a large jug/pitcher or 4 tall glasses and pour in the elderflower cordial. Top up with sparkling water, garnish with a few elderflowers, if using, and serve.

ginger beer, lime and mint crush

This is a delicious and unusual soft drink that everyone will love. For adults only, try adding vodka to make a very special Moscow mule.

2 limes, each cut into 8 wedges
a handful of fresh mint sprigs
1 teaspoon caster/superfine sugar
ice cubes
500 ml/2 cups ginger beer

Serves 2

Place the lime, mint and sugar in a glass jug and, using a wooden muddler, crush the ingredients together lightly.

Add plenty of ice cubes, top up with ginger beer and pour into 2 tall glasses to serve.

lemon drop

There are various ways to present this shooter. You can coat a lemon slice in sugar and lay it over the surface of the glass to bite into after the shot, or you can take it one step further and soak the lemon in Cointreau before coating it, then set it alight!

3½ tablespoons lemon vodka
1 tablespoon Cointreau
1⅓ tablespoons fresh lemon juice
lemon slices, to garnish

Serves 2

Add all the ingredients except the lemon slices to a shaker filled with ice. Shake very hard and strain into shot glasses. Garnish each with a lemon slice.

lemon sherbet

Old cookbooks are full of thirst-quenching drinks like this one: a simple recipe for old-fashioned lemonade, which tastes gorgeous and is totally revitalizing.

Wrap half the lemon zest in plastic wrap and reserve for later use. Put the remaining zest and the lemon juice in a large heatproof jug/pitcher with the sugar cubes/lumps. Add the boiling water and stir, then cover and leave to cool. Strain and refrigerate. Serve in tall glasses with the lemon slices, a few strips of the reserved lemon zest and ice cubes.

VARIATION
Serve in glasses poured over 2 tablespoons of chopped summer fruit.

thinly pared zest and freshly squeezed juice of 4 unwaxed lemons
90 g/3¼ oz. sugar cubes/lumps
1 litre/4 cups boiling water

TO SERVE
1 lemon, sliced
8 ice cubes

Makes 1 litre/4 cups

sea freeze

This non-alcoholic refresher is a play on the classic cranberry, grapefruit and vodka cocktail Sea Breeze, but with the cranberry juice frozen into ice cubes.

300 ml/1¼ cups cranberry juice
400 ml/1⅔ cups fresh grapefruit juice
old-fashioned lemonade
lime slices, to garnish

Serves 2

Pour the cranberry juice into an ice-cube tray and freeze for at least 4 hours.

Divide the cubes between 2 tall glasses and add the fresh grapefruit juice. Top up with lemonade and garnish with slices of lime to serve.

strawberry iced tea

Pretty-in-pink is a good way of describing this fragrant and mouth-watering concoction, so perfect for a pre-dinner drink on a balmy summer evening.

2 tablespoons strawberry-flavoured tea infusion
1 vanilla bean, split lengthways
1 litre/4 cups just-boiled water
2 tablespoons rosewater
ice cubes
250 g/2 cups strawberries, hulled and sliced
clear sparkling lemonade
rose petals, to garnish (optional)

Serves 6

Place the strawberry tea and vanilla bean in a heatproof jug/pitcher and add the just-boiled water. Stir well and leave to steep until cold. Strain the tea into a clean jug and stir in the rosewater.

Put a few ice cubes into 6 tall glasses, add some strawberries and pour over the tea. Top up with lemonade and garnish with a few rose petals, if using, to serve.

cranberry and fruit punch

This colourful, fruity punch will delight children and adults alike. Of course, for those who just love a little extra pizzazz, you could always add a shot or two of vodka!

250 g/2 cups mixed fresh berries, such as strawberries, raspberries and blueberries
1 orange, sliced
2 litres/8 cups cranberry juice
1 small cucumber, peeled, deseeded and sliced
sparkling mineral/soda water or clear sparkling lemonade
ice cubes, to serve

Serves 12

Put the berries, orange slices and cranberry juice in a large jug/pitcher and chill for 1 hour.

When ready to serve, add the cucumber and some ice and top up with sparkling water. Pour into tall glasses or tumblers to serve.

index

recipe credits

VALERIE AIKMAN-SMITH
Candied Salted Almonds
Watermelon and Ricotta Salata Salad

GHILLIE BASAN
Lamb and Porcini Skewers with Sage
   and Parmesan
Stuffed Chargrilled Sardines
Summer Vegetable Skewers with
   Home-made Pesto

FIONA BECKETT
Feta, Cucumber and Mint Spring Salad
Grape and Lemon Mascarpone Tart
Quick Mini Pissaladieres
Red Pepper and Manchego Tortilla
Steak Niçoise
Strawberry Tiramisu
Tuscan-style Steak

JULZ BERESFORD
Marinated Anchovies
Minted Pea Soup with Frazzled Prosciutto
Pizzette with Assorted Meaty and Veggie
   Toppings
Potatoes in Spicy Sauce

MAXINE CLARK
Baby Asparagus with Vinaigrette and
   Chopped Egg
Barbecued Salmon Steaks with Basil
   and Parmesan Butter
Creamy Tomato and Bread Soup with
   Basil Oil
Fennel and Black Olive Risotto
Grilled Mixed Vegetable Salad with
   Balsamic Herb Dressing
Grilled Sardines
Insalata Nizzarda
Orange, Endive and Black Olive Salad
Pizza Alla Margherita
Seafood Salad with Lemon and Parsley
Lemon Sorbet
Sicilian Spaghetti with Tomato Sauce
Tiramisù
Tomato Upside-down Tart with Basil
Vanilla Gelato

ROSS DOBSON
Affogato Parfait
Garlic Olive Oil, Warm Marinated Olives
   and Serrano Ham Platter
Heirloom Tomato, Burrata and Basil
   Summer Salad
Lemon and Herb Chicken with Roasted
   Vegetables
Linguini with Clams and Garlic
Messy Strawberries Romanoff
Parmesan Crackers
Spiced Muscat Figs
Spicy Pasta Salad with Tuna and Feta
Spicy Sausage and Pepper Pizza with
   Rocket Salad
Summer Fruit Compote with
   Zabaglione
White Sangria

CLARE FERGUSON
Asparagus with Prosciutto
Caponata
Deep-fried Baby Artichokes
Seafood Antipasti with Parsley
   and Lemon
Greek Chicken Stifado
Mediterranean Fish Soup
Pan-Fried Green Peppers
Pan-fried Halloumi

Pork Filet with Marsala
Provençal Fish Soup
Provence-style Artichokes with Bacon
Radicchio with Gorgonzola and Walnuts
Sisteron-style Roast Lamb
Souvlaki in Pita
Spanish Clams with Ham
Stuffed Baby Vegetables
Stuffed Greek Aubergines/Eggplant
Tapenade

LIZ FRANKLIN
Ajo Blanco
Balsamic Ice Cream
Mixed Griddled Fish with Romesco
   Sauce

TONIA GEORGE
Chicken Avgolemono

JENNIFER JOYCE
Celeriac Rémoulade
Saffron and Garlic Aioli
Seafood Salad with Dill
Smoky Aubergine/Eggplant Dip
Spicy Baked Feta
Swordfish Souvlaki Bites

ELSA PETERSEN-SCHEPELERN
Peaches and Sauternes Ice Cream

LOUISE PICKFORD
Barbecued Artichokes
Barbecued Courgettes/Zucchini
Barbecued Fish Bathed in Oregano and
   Lemon
Bean Salad with Mint and Parmesan
Berries with Honeyed Yogurt
Butterflied Lamb with White Bean Salad
Caipirinha
Classic Sangria
Cranberry and Fruit Punch
Elderflower and Berry Cup
Focaccia Topped with Cherry Tomatoes
   and Pesto
Fresh Figs with Vin Santo and
   Mascarpone
Frothy Iced Coffee
Ginger Beer, Lime and Mint Crush
Iced Pear Sparkle
Mixed Mushroom Frittata
Mojito
Olive-infused Chicken with Charred
   Lemons
Onion, Thyme and Goat Cheese Tarts
Open Chicken Burgers with Grilled
   Vegetables
Grilled Polenta Triangles
Pan Bagnat
Pasta, Squash and Feta Salad with Olive
   Dressing
Peach and Strawberry Sangria
Roquefort and Walnut Tart
Sage-rubbed Pork Chops
Sea Freeze
Simple Tomato and Olive Tart with
   Parmesan
Souvlaki with Bulgur Wheat Salad
Spanish-style Skewers
Steak with Blue Cheese Butter
Strawberry Iced Tea
Stuffed Picnic Loaf
Summer Leaf and Herb Salad
Whole Chicken Roasted on the Barbecue

BEN REED
Lemon Drop

ANNIE RIGG
Alioli
Arancini with Pecorino, Porcini &
   Mozzarella
Assorted Focaccia Crostini
Chorizo & Olives in Red Wine with
   Padrón Peppers
Crispy Calamari with Beans & Chorizo

RENA SALAMAN
Fresh Mussels with Saffron and Lemon
Fried Meatballs
Grilled Tuna Skewers
Pork with Quinces
Spicy Chicken Skewers
Spicy Meat Pastries
Spinach and Cheese Pie
Tomato, Cucumber, Onion and
   Feta Salad
Traditional Cheese Pies
Vegetable Fritters

FIONA SMITH
Farmhouse Terrine
Greek Barley Salad
Ham and Chicken Pots with Cornichons
Hummus
Tuna and Cannellini Bean Salad
Tzatziki

LINDA TUBBY
Gazpacho
Soupe Verdon

FRAN WARDE
Avocado and Chickpea Salad
Baked Aubergine/Eggplant with Pesto
   Sauce
Barbecued Prawns/Shrimp with Lemon
Cafe Frappe
Cheesy Stuffed Croissants
Chicken Salad Wrap
Easy Fish Stew
Espresso Granita
Fruit Platter
Mozzarella Baked Salad
Salad Box
Strawberry Tart
Sweet Glazed Pepper Salad
Swordfish with Salsa
Tumeric Lamb Fillet with Couscous
   Salad
Watermelon Vodka
White Wine Spritzer

LAURA WASHBURN
Provençal Tian with Tomato Sauce
Chicory Salad with Roquefort, Celery and
   Walnuts
Fresh Fruit Tart
Goat Cheese Tart
Napoléons with Lemon Cream
Prawns/Shrimp with Garlic
Tomato Salad with Anchovy Vinaigrette
Vegetable Bouillabaisse
Whole Roast Monkfish

LINDY WILDSMITH
Bruschetta with Baby Mozzarella and
   Cherry Tomatoes
Catalan Salad with Tuna and Aioli
Lemon Sherbet
Nectarines in Sambuca and Lime Juice
Pannacotta Galliano with Summer Fruit
   Compote
Risotto with Sicilian Pesto
Sicilian-style Lamb Cutlets

---

photography credits

Key: a=above, b=below, r=right, l=left,
c=centre.

JAN BALDWIN
Pages 43 l, 169 l, 173 r (house in Cape
Elizabeth designed by Stephen Blatt
Architects)

**CAROLYN BARBER AND
EMMA MITCHELL**
Page 13 b

STEVE BAXTER
Pages 34 l, 35 r, 68 b and a, 98–99, 103 b

MARTIN BRIGDALE
Pages 1, 26 r, 36 r, 48 a, 51 r, 57 r, 63 a,
65, 69, 71 b, 72 l, 73 b, 76 l, 84 r, 94 l, 97,
118 r, 119, 121 r, 122 r, 123 r, 124 l, 126a,
132, 133r, 136 l, 138 l, 139 r, 142, 144,
145 l, 150 r, 155, 156 b, 159 b, 160 l, 171

DAVID BRITTAIN
Pages 83 l, 151 a

PETER CASSIDY
Pages 4, 8, 9 ac, 9 ar, 10-11, 12 r, 13 a,
17 l, 18, 19 l, 20–23, 24 r, 25 l, 27 r,
28–30, 33 ar, 34 r, 35 l, 38–42, 43 r,
44–45 a, 55 a, 60 r, 66–67, 70, 74 a, 75 l,
93 ac, 101 r, 102 b, 105, 106 l, 108, 110 l,
112, 117 ar, 120 r, 121 l, 122 l, 127,
140–141, 153, 154, 158

CHRISTOPHER DRAKE
Pages 3, 54 r (Maurizio Epifani, owner
of L'Oro dei Farlocchi), 88 ar, 93 al, 123 l,
134 (Enrica Stabile's house, Le Thor,
Provence), 137 r (Mireille and Jean Claude
Lothon, La Cour Beaudeval Antiquities,
4 Rue des Fontaines, 28210 Faverolles,
France, +33 2 37 51 47 67), 138 ar, 145 r
(Giorgio Irene Silvagni's house in Provence;
wire 'presentoir', l'Utile e il Dilettevole;
green pottery, Irene Silvagni's collection)

MELANIE ECLARE
Pages 87 br (Laura Cooper & Nick
Taggart's Los Angeles garden designed
by Cooper/Taggart Designs), 95 a (Nancy
Goslee Power, garden designer), 114al
(Laura Cooper & Nick Taggart's Los
Angeles garden designed by Cooper/Taggart
Designs), 163 r, (Laura Cooper & Nick
Taggart's Los Angeles garden designed
by Cooper/Taggart Designs)

DANIEL FARMER
Pages 110r

JONATHAN GREGSON
Pages 59 l

RICHARD JUNG
Pages 32, 47 ac, 60 l, 61–62, 79, 86,
87 a, 91 r, 139 l, 160 br, 161 r

TOM LEIGHTON
Pages 138 br

WILLIAM LINGWOOD
Pages 165–166, 169 r, 170, 172, 173 l

PAUL MASSEY
Pages 6, 19 c (The Dodo;
www.thedodo.co.uk), 19 br (Jane Packer's
home in Suffolk), 71 ac, 82 bc, 103 a (the
home of Charlotte Lynggaard in Denmark,
designer of olelynggaard.dk), 117ac

DIANA MILLER
Pages 14, 15 a, 36 c, 53, 54 left, 55 c,
56, 57 l

WILLIAM REAVELL
Pages 156 background

CLAIRE RICHARDSON
Page 114ar (Chateau de Christin,
Chambres d'Hotes de Luxe, Reception-
Seminaires), 134

MARK SCOTT
Pages 16, 47 ar, 91 left, 96 l (Cyrene,
www.greekhabitat.com), 96r (Villa Io), 107
(Cyrene, www.greekhabitat.com), 113 l,
136 r

YUKI SUGIURA
Page 64

LUCINDA SYMONS
Page 160 ar

DEBI TRELOAR
Pages 9 al, 19 ar, 26 l, 27 bl, 27 al, 33 br,
47 al, 47 b, 51 bl, 55 b, 58ar, 59 br, 71 al,
72 r, 76 r, 78, 82 bl, 82 r, 84 l, 85, 88 al,
88 ac, 95 bl, 101 l, 104 b, 114 bl, 117 b
& al, 125, 128, 130–131, 133 l, 138 c, 143
ac & ar, 146 b, 149 l, 152 a (available for
location hire at www.shootspaces.com),
152 b, 157, 161 l, 162 l, 163 l, 164,
167 a, 168

PIA TRYDE
Pages 12 l (Jane Cumberbatch's house,
Los Cepellines), 17 r, 33 l (Jane
Cumberbatch's house, Los Cepellines),
115 r (Jane Cumberbatch's house, Los
Cepellines), 36 l, 118 l, 151 br, 156 a

CHRIS TUBBS
Pages 2 (Giorgio and Ilaria Miani's
Podere Casellacce in Val d'Orcia), 24 l
(a house in Maremma, Tuscany designed
by Contemporanea), 25 r (Vanni and
Nicoletta Calamai's home near Siena), 50
(Gabriella Cantaluppi Abbado's home in
Monticchiello), 63 b (Toia Saibene and
Giuliana Magnifico's home in Lucignano,
Tuscany), 68 l (Giorgio and Ilaria Miani's
Podere Casellacce in Val d'Orcia)

SIMON UPTON
Pages 126 b (Bruno & Hélène Lafforgue,
Mas de l'Ange, Maison d'Hôte, Petite route
de St. Remy-de-Provence, 13946
Mollégès, France)

IAN WALLACE
Pages 5 b, 15 a, 46, 49, 71 ar, 73 a, 74 b,
75 r, 77, 80–81, 82 al, 83 r, 87 bl, 88 b,
90, 92, 93 b, 93 ar, 94 r, 95 br, 100,102 a,
104 a, 106 r, 111, 113 r, 115 l, 137 l, 143
al & 143b, 146 l, 148, front and back
endpapers.

KATE WHITAKER
Pages 5 a, 9 b, 31, 37, 52, 116, 120 l,
135, 147, 149 r, 150 l, 151 bl, 167 b

PENNY WINCER
Page 162 r

POLLY WREFORD
Pages 48 b, 159 a (Johann Nilsson and
Ulrika Rudolph-Hall, Stenhuset Antikhandel
shop, café and B&B in Stockamollan,
Sweden, www.stenhusetantikhandel.com)